To

MW01235080

WINDOW TO GOD
A Physician's Spiritual Pilgrimage

From one ray
of Light to
another.

Best wishes,

WINDOW TO GOD
A Physician's Spiritual Pilgrimage

A Medical and Scientific Look
at the Special Gifts
of Edgar Cayce

T. Lee Baumann, M.D.

ASSOCIATION FOR
RESEARCH AND
ENLIGHTENMENT

A.R.E. Press • Virginia Beach • Virginia

A.R.E. Press
215 67th Street
Virginia Beach, VA 23451-2061

Library of Congress Cataloguing-in-Publication Data
Baumann, T. Lee, 1950-
    Window to God : a medical and scientific look at the special gifts of Edgar Cayce / by T. Lee Baumann.
        p.   cm.
    ISBN 0-87604-506-9 (trade pbk.)
    1. Cayce, Edgar, 1877-1945. 2. Psychics–United States. 3. Parapsychol-ogy–Religious aspects 4. Parapsychology and science. I. Title.
    BF1027.C3B38 2005
    133.8'092–dc22

                                        2005008540

The author is grateful for permission to use excerpts from the following works:
    Edgar Cayce Readings 1971, 1993, 1994, 1995, and 1996 by the Edgar Cayce Foundation. All rights reserved.
    Revised Standard Version of the Bible. © 1952 by the Division of Christian Education of the National Council of the Churches of Christ in the United States of America. Used by Permission. All rights reserved.

Edgar Cayce Readings © 1971, 1993, 1994, 1995, 1996
by the Edgar Cayce Foundation.
All rights reserved.

Cover design by Richard Boyle

This book is dedicated to everyone seeking an
understanding of life's purpose.

I especially wish to thank my wife, Brenda, and my son,
Morgan, for their unrelenting support.

Contents

Preface

I remain appreciative that the Association for Research and Enlightenment (A.R.E.) chose to publish my first book, *God at the Speed of Light: The Melding of Science and Spirituality*, a purely scientific text dealing with spirituality and sharing the common ties to the Cayce legacy of energy, light, the nature of reality, and God. I owe my most sincere gratitude to Brenda English, the senior editor at the A.R.E. responsible for the successful end result. As a first-time author, I must thank Brenda for getting the manuscript to its final destination.

God at the Speed of Light is a scientific thesis that documents the intimate relationship between God and physical light and, hence, the verification of a higher intelligence in the universe. When the A.R.E. published the book in the spring of 2002, I had only the faintest idea of who Edgar Cayce was. As I actively engaged in the promotion of the book over the succeeding years, I had the pleasure to meet countless A.R.E. members who discussed Cayce with me at length.[1] As I familiarized myself more with Edgar Cayce, my spiritual path took a new direction, ultimately leading to the publication of the manuscript you are reading now.

The A.R.E., which together with the Cayce hospital is the consummation of Edgar Cayce's life work, publishes various spiritual books, the majority of which relate either directly or indirectly to Cayce's beliefs or his voluminous readings.[2]

Since first being introduced to Edgar Cayce's story, I have become a member of the A.R.E. community, and it has been a wonderful and rewarding experience.

Window to God represents a continuation of my evolving spiritual journey and my continued research into light and the afterlife. As you will see, Edgar Cayce plays a crucial role in this pilgrimage.

My life's experiences and readings have introduced me to many individuals with unique and fascinating stories. Upon first reading about Edgar Cayce, the great American clairvoyant, I found that his story captured my spiritual and scientific heart. *Window to God* is a study of his special gift and the credibility of his profound physical and life readings. For those unfamiliar with Edgar Cayce, the term *reading* refers to Cayce's verbalization while in one of his self-induced hypnotic trances. He could place himself into these meditative states at will. He performed primarily two types of readings: the more numerous physical (or medical) readings and the life (or spiritual) readings. Clients typically requested physical readings for diagnoses and advice on how to improve their mental and physical health.

When Cayce gave a life reading, however, he did not directly address medical issues but rather assisted the recipient in understanding life in terms of past incarnations and astrologic influences. To illustrate, an individual may have requested a life reading to better understand why he or she had developed polio. The life reading would answer this question.

The number of physical readings far exceeded the number of life readings. The Edgar Cayce Foundation reports that the total number of all readings is 14,306, of which 1,920 are life readings and 9,603 are physical readings.[3] Each type of reading had enormous import but for vastly different reasons. In Chapter 3, I discuss these differences in detail.

From a personal perspective, Edgar Cayce has made a major impact on my life. Because of his incredible life story and my continuing research, I have come to accept and defend the concept of reincarnation—a concept that Cayce advocated and that is covertly discussed and defended in the Bible (Chapter 8)!

Throughout this document, you will find that I utilize various resources—including the Cayce readings—to support the concepts that I discuss. These resources include scientific and experimental data, medical references, quantum physics texts, the major religious manuscripts of the world (including the Bible), and even some scientifically supported and corroborated, albeit "paranormal," phenomena. Among the latter, I include citations from multiple well-researched near-death experiences (NDEs). I am of the conviction that NDEs are *not* hallucinatory phenomena caused from drugs, illness, or oxygen deprivation—they are real. There are just too many NDEs of young, healthy individuals in whom the above conditions were not a factor. In these individuals, CPR was instituted immediately and, obviously, successfully. Yet their NDEs were no different and no less real than those of patients in whom any or all of those conditions were operative. Further, corroborative elements from innumerable, well-documented NDEs abound in the literature. Since the Cayce readings also fall within the general category of the paranormal, I think you will find that the readings and the NDE citations appropriately complement one another.

Window to God represents one additional consequence of my life's quest to answer life's eternal questions, such as "Why are we here? What is the purpose to life? What happens after death?" The story of Edgar Cayce represents one important stepping-stone in this enterprise. As such, it is important that the reader have an understanding of some of the notations in this book. Edgar Cayce utilized a filing system to organize his more than 14,000 readings. He is, beyond a doubt, the most well-documented psychic in world history. A stenographer, usually Gladys Davis, recorded each hypnotic session. Each individual for whom a reading was given received a number, for example "5237." The first reading for this person received the designation of 5237-1, the second reading, 5237-2, etc. Unless otherwise noted, I have referenced each reading following its quoted excerpt.

Special Note: I must caution the reader with a necessary disclaimer. Do not employ any remedy cited in this text or the Cayce readings without first consulting your current medical practitioner. Many of the medical recommendations mentioned are antiquated and can no longer be endorsed. Although they may have been appropriate during Cayce's era, and/or for the particular patient for whom the reading was intended, safer and more effective therapies may now exist or be more appropriate for you.

1

My Introduction to Edgar Cayce

*T*he first year following the publication of *God at the Speed of Light*, I toured the country and met innumerable, fascinating people— many of them A.R.E. members. My initial impression was that A.R.E. members were a select number of very spiritual people, many with their own personal experiences with the paranormal. Others were well versed in alternative medicine. Most members tended to be believers in God, as was Cayce. Many believed in God based upon faith alone. A great number, however, were spiritual believers, the result of transformations by wondrous psychic or metaphysical experiences, including the near–death experience. I came to the greater understanding that the A.R.E. exists as the rare organization where people of all beliefs and backgrounds feel free and comfortable to express their rare experiences without fear of criticism, judgment, or stereotyping.

My first real interaction with A.R.E. members occurred September 27, 2002, in Houston. This was the site of my first workshop dealing with *God at the Speed of Light*. I loved it! The attendees viewed my book and presentations as complementary to their own beliefs. Most of the people present in Houston had witnessed or experienced supernatural phenomena in their own lives. (Imagine trying to relate these types of experiences to your co-workers, friends, or even some close family members!) These people would have become the laughable targets of their colleagues and friends. The A.R.E. often attracts such individuals due to the very fact that they are welcome there and even encouraged to share their experiences with others. At the A.R.E., such experiences are the norm. Granted, I don't agree with all their beliefs, but then again, neither do they demand or expect it of you. The A.R.E. is a melting pot of exceptional concepts, alternative medicine, and phenomenal people, literally. The vast majority of members are sincere in their beliefs, accepting of new ideas, and unhesitant to express their views.

This was the state of my world when I traveled to Louisiana on March 13, 2003. I was headed to New Orleans for a short workshop in the neighboring town of Metairie, hosted by the A.R.E. team coordinator for southeast Louisiana.

Marlene Duet was my most welcoming host, and her home was my home for the weekend. Not only was this an exceptionally rewarding time for me (and, hopefully, also the workshop attendees), but I benefited from Marlene's extraordinary knowledge of Edgar Cayce. Prior to this, I knew that Edgar Cayce was a gifted, spiritual individual who shared his rare gift of divination by benefiting those in need. His fascinating story is the topic of countless books on the market today. (For those interested, the A.R.E. bookstore offers them—check www.edgarcayce.org—you do not have to be a member.) Marlene taught me more about Edgar Cayce than anyone ever had. I left New Orleans with two of the best-known books ever published on this unbelievable man—*The Story of Edgar Cayce: There Is a River*[4] by Thomas Sugrue (A.R.E. Press) and *Edgar Cayce: An American Prophet*[5] by Sidney Kirkpatrick (Riverhead Books). Kirkpatrick had also visited and stayed with Marlene when he was in the New Orleans area. By the time I left New Orleans, I had read most of *There Is a River* and my views on clairvoyance were changed forever.

What impressed me most about Edgar Cayce's life was his devotion to his God and Christ, and his humility. He repeatedly turned down opportunities to financially exploit his gift as a clairvoyant healer, and, in doing so, spent most of his life in poverty. Cayce considered it a sin to turn away those in need just because they couldn't pay. He attempted in every way to emulate Christ's life in helping others. Another aspect of Cayce, which made him appear all the more like one of us, was his own initial doubt as to the validity of his own readings. Most of us can identify with our own skepticism of many known psychics. As such, it was meaningful to me to see that Cayce was no different. He was the first to state that he did not understand his gift. He admitted that he did not understand the substance of most of his physical (medical) readings and did not agree with or even accept several of his life (spiritual and past-life) readings. It took Cayce and his family years before they came to finally accept the notion of reincarnation and its role in our current lives (for example, karma).

From a personal standpoint, I had never found any consistency in the Bible regarding divine justice. Most religious scholars accept an "eye for an eye" as an example of delayed retribution, meaning that mortals await death or the final judgment to observe God's justice. The theme was this: If we lead our lives according to God's (or Christ's) specifications despite life's injustices, we will ultimately be rewarded in Heaven. For most of my life, it remained difficult for me to accept this premise. As a physician, I bore witness to children and other innocents who endured indescribable suffering or succumbed to illness or trauma for no apparent divine reason. We read in the news, on a daily basis, of heinous crimes committed on people of any age, sex, race, religion, and station in life. Surely, not all these people were so sinful and deserving of celestial retribution to deserve these carnal punishments. For me, Cayce changed my thinking about all that. Suddenly, karma and reincarnation explained all the concepts of divine justice inherent and purposely obscured in the Bible (after the church declared these doctrines to be heresy[6]). The concepts of karma and reincarnation dictate that those of us presently alive on earth are in our current predicament as the result of past mistakes—not good fortune! We are resuming life on this planet to learn the lessons that we failed to learn in our first or previous lifetime(s). So how did Cayce, the son of a simple store manager, come to such notoriety? The story is one of pain, poverty, and promise.

Edgar Cayce was born near Hopkinsville, Kentucky, on March 18, 1877. At the age of 13, the young Edgar had his first episode of divination, wherein he found that he could learn his school lessons by merely sleeping on his books! It was not until age 24, however, that Edgar performed his first reading. Edgar had lost his voice in the months previous, and multiple treatment attempts had proved futile. In desperation, Cayce allowed a local hypnotist to lead him into a trance. This episode of hypnosis proved successful when Edgar verbally diagnosed and treated his own condition while under hypnosis. Edgar soon learned that he could go into the hypnotic state on his own. In this condition, he found he could diagnose the conditions of people anywhere in the world and recommend appropriate treatment. His story may well have ended there, except for the degree to which his extraordinary ability was documented. Beginning in 1923, Gladys Davis, his stenographer, transcribed most of the 14,000 readings. Cayce would typically send one copy to the patient and keep one copy for his own records. The extent of archiving was an enormous achievement, and it remains one of the greatest attributes of the Cayce legacy.

For each reading, Cayce required that the patient be at a specified location at a specific time. On several occasions while in trance, Cayce was unable to locate "the body" of the individual requesting diagnosis and treatment—that is, the person was not at the designated location. Edgar would often (although not always) ascertain exactly why the person was not present. When the individual was subsequently contacted as to his or her whereabouts, Cayce's information would prove accurate.[7] The stories of corroboration are included in the countless Edgar Cayce books available, as well as in the readings, and they are incredible and fascinating. Despite the obvious power inherent in Cayce's ability, the "Source" of the information (while in trance) would not disclose facts that could be used for any personal gain. This omniscient Source of the Cayce information is also referred to as the Akashic Records. It represents the spiritual spring of knowledge from which Cayce retrieved his information. This wealth of knowledge could potentially have made Cayce a rich man. Nonetheless, Cayce's religious convictions, along with inducement from the Source, prevented him and his family from profiting from this faculty. When Edgar Cayce passed away in 1945, the value of his entire estate, including his home, came to less than $10,000.[8]

In the next chapter, we will examine scientifically how it is possible that this rare faculty of clairvoyance can exist.

2

Contemplation on Clairvoyance

We do not have to look far to realize that our five human senses are quite limited, though invaluable, in experiencing our universe. NASA has sophisticated telescopes and satellites capable of perceiving X-ray, infrared, and other non-visible forms of light radiation. Astronomers have evidence that there exist various forms of dark matter in the universe that we, despite our technological advances, are currently incapable of detecting. There is much in our universe that we cannot perceive.

I have been raised and trained in the scientific method. This approach requires that experimentation prove the correctness of any scientific theory before the scientific community can accept it. Thus, if a hypothesis cannot be proven in the research laboratory, it remains theory, not fact. Most of my education was influenced by the persuasion of the scientific method. Despite being raised as a Christian, my mentors and educators led me into the respected scientific direction. Early in my childhood, I attended a Christian summer camp in Wisconsin. My cabin counselor, on his own initiative, lectured the young campers in my cabin, nightly, on why there was not a God. I remember one night when he displayed a flask of liquid that fluoresced with a bluish glow in the total darkness of the cabin. He noted that this exhibition was not unlike the process observed in fireflies. Scientific researchers could duplicate this accomplishment—God was not required. God was, he noted, purely an abstraction manufactured by humans to allay their fears regarding death. Thus, even at this early age, my initial doubts on the existence of God were created. Subsequently, my continuing education as a premedical student in college and ensuing medical training only enhanced my conviction in the scientific method and my skepticism toward God.

As humans, we tend to accept as fact those occurrences that we can see. Sight represents our most important instrument of verification. Senses falling outside of this realm are subject to more scrutiny. If we walk through the front door and smell cinnamon–flavored apples, do we assume that an apple pie is baking in the oven? Perhaps, but we reserve the possibility that a potpourri, scented candle, or spray air freshener is the source of the fragrance. Similar examples exist for touch, taste, and hearing. I have wandered throughout my home, trying to find the origin of a crash that I've heard. Similarly, did that cry I heard come from my indoor cat or a commotion outside? Our senses are fraught with frailties. We tend to lend most credence to our sense of sight. Those without the gift of sight enhance their circumstances by relying upon their remaining four senses. As such, most blind persons would have little trouble distinguishing sensations that might confuse the rest of us (for example, those cited above). These examples hardly hint at the hidden dimensions that likely exist beyond our senses.

When I gave my presentation in Metairie, Louisiana, in 2003, I included a talk on "Hidden Dimensions." In this presentation I discussed how science, specifically the string theories of quantum physics, offers support for the existence of concealed dimensions. As I drove home following the workshop, I realized that I already had an explanation for Cayce's unique gift. I knew that I didn't have a complete understanding of the science involved, but I was going to pursue it. Simultaneously, I would learn more about this unusual man and his celebrated ability. This research would require access to all of the Cayce readings. Marlene had already educated me that Cayce's readings are available through three sources: (1) the A.R.E. library in Virginia Beach, Virginia, (2) the

Internet (for A.R.E. members), and (3) CD–ROM of the readings (sold through the A.R.E. Bookstore). With these resources, I began my new journey of enlightenment.

SCIENCE OFFERS AN EXPLANATION

Quantum theory is the concept that leads us to the very real probability of concealed realms and ultimately an explanation for clairvoyance. To explore this theory, we should start with the classic model of the atom (Figure 1):

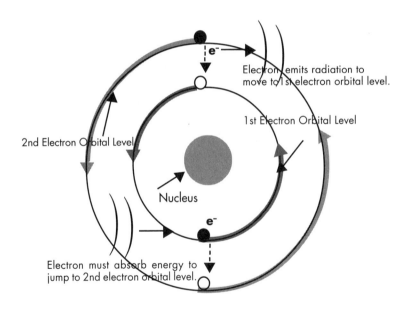

Figure 1. Standard model of the atom

Although physicists now describe this model as outdated (I will explain why), it is the classic example by which most of us learned about the atom. We see in the figure that light is intimately associated with the electrons and, hence, all atoms and molecules. Electrons are constantly exchanging photons. When a photon strikes an electron, it imparts energy to the electron, causing it to vault to a higher orbital level. In a similar vein, the only way for an electron to descend to a lower orbit is to emit a photon. Through this figure, it is not difficult to understand the intrinsic and necessary role that light plays in all matter. Light will continue to re-emerge as a significant feature in this text, playing an important role in clairvoyance. For the present, let us examine further this depiction of the atom.

What are shown as points or dots in Figure 1 (e.g., the electrons) are meant to represent small points in space—in other words, particles. We now recognize that these points are merely schematic representations of entities (for lack of a better term) that may exist as *either* waves or particles (hence, the wave–particle duality). It is now accepted, through the Copenhagen interpretation of quantum mechanics, that all such points (and subsequently all matter) exist as waves in their natural unobserved state. Strangely, science has shown that it is the act of human observation that causes the waves to collapse into particles.[9] Therefore, it is as particles that we humans experience what we designate as reality. As a simplistic example, our eyes cannot directly detect light waves. Rather, the expansive light waves strike our retinas, where they then collapse into discrete particles. This action stimulates the rods or cones of our retinas. The resulting signals to our brain allow our conscious mind to convert the consequent chemistry into coordinated dots of color, forming a recognizable pattern and image.

The above classic model of the atom plays a central role in scientists' search for a *theory of everything* or *final theory*. For decades, physicists have attempted to integrate the four forces or laws of nature into a single theory. These four forces include the weak nuclear force of the atom (the force involved in radioactivity), the strong nuclear force (which holds quarks together to form nuclear particles), the electromagnetic force (for example, magnetic force fields), and gravity. We can appreciate the strength of these forces through the knowledge that most of matter is space. Yet this space of the atomic and molecular structure is, for the most part, impenetrable—the result of these atomic forces. Simply put, this is why we cannot walk through walls.

The standard model, which we discussed, and most other models of the atom have been able to merge the first three of the above named forces, but not gravity. The failure to incorporate gravity into the various models has been the cause of their downfall. Currently, the most promising theory for the ultimate union of gravity with the other forces is string theory. String theory describes the smallest possible constituents of the atom as vibrating strings or loops, rather than point-particles. What is remarkable about this group of theories is not only the potential incorporation of gravity with the other three forces but the mandate for the existence of either ten (for the superstring) or twenty-six total dimensions (for the bosonic string theory). The numbers ten and twenty-six include the dimension of time, so the purely spatial dimensions are nine and twenty-five respectively.

If we accept the concept of the obligatory, extra dimensions of the string theories, then the question demanding an answer becomes "What constitutes these extra dimensions?" I suggest that these accessory realms contain at least some of the supernatural domains of the paranormal. Examples would include the provinces of déjà vu, the collective unconscious, Akashic Records, psychic knowledge and visions, clairvoyance, dreams, near-death experiences, out-of-body experiences, etc.

Dannion Brinkley's near-death experience (*Saved by the Light*[10]) is just one of a multitude of NDEs that exemplify the veracity of this realm of knowledge in the near-death domain. In his unique encounter, unlike most other NDEs, "Beings of Light" imparted to Brinkley knowledge and prophecies of future events, which he retained even after his return to the body. Many of the predictions have already come to pass, including the election of Ronald Reagan as president, the nuclear disaster at Chernobyl, and the collapse of the Soviet Union.

If we acknowledge the likelihood that at least some paranormal, psychic, or other supernatural phenomena truly occur, then quantum theory gives us a possible scientific explanation. As a physician, I have to include one additional possibility: the hallucinatory realm. From my many years in medical practice, I have witnessed far too many indi-

viduals labeled as mentally ill or senile. I believe the majority of these
patients were, indeed, truly psychotic or demented from the medical
standpoint. However, I must also admit to examining the occasional
patient in whom something more appeared to be transpiring. This was
the sporadic individual who visualized or spoke to deceased loved ones
or persons unknown. Who was I to question that this person was not
seeing or hearing something or someone beyond my own power of
perception and comprehension? Even today we accept and applaud
many psychics whom we would have run out of town a century ago. It
appears that society is more open-minded than ever before, and I interpret this change as a positive one. Sanity currently represents a label
that merely identifies those of us with secure bonds to our particulate,
four-dimensional environment.

Let us begin our examination of the Cayce readings by reviewing the
Source's assessment of various cases of mental illness. In the excerpt
that follows, the term *dementia praecox* is an outdated designation for
schizophrenia:

> EC: Yes, we have the body, [5344].
> There has already been departure of the soul, which
> only waits by here. We have the physical being but the
> control of same only needs the care, the attention, the
> greater love which may be shown in and under the
> circumstances, which will give the best conditions for this
> body. For already there are those weakenings so of the
> centers of the cerebrospinal system that no physical help,
> as we find, may be administered, only the mental or soul
> help as will be a part of the mental or superconscious self.
> This condition has come from pressures which caused
> dementia praecox.   5344-1

Thus, Cayce knew, in at least some psychotic afflictions, that the soul
had access to the hidden, spiritual dimensions through its ability to
abandon the body. Or was the Source implying that the soul had lost all
contact with the body and mind—not unlike clinical brain death? Or
both?

At least some mental illness cases probed by Cayce's clairvoyance fell
into yet another separate category—possession:

Yes, we have the body-mind here, [2865]. As we find, there are physical or pathological, as well as mental-psychological, disturbances. These, while they do not work together, are caused or produced by retentions in the mind—or that which is partially, or at times, possession.

. . . we would begin subjugating the body-mind by suggestion—or hypnosis. Such an [sic] one as Dr. Kuhn . . . may be risked with this undertaking . . .

After there has been gained control of the body once or twice (by hypnosis), begin the use of the low Wet Cell Appliance . . .

These low electrical forces will aid in eliminating the tendencies for possession. Sufficient electrical forces are created. 2865-1

From these excerpts, we see that mental illness may represent a complex aggregation of possible afflictions, with varying interpretations. The examples cited include departure of the soul as well as possession of the body by discarnate spirits, in addition to all the modern–day medical explanations. Unfortunately, even with recent scientific advances, the present–day medical community is only on the threshold of understanding this all–too–common group of disorders.

With at least some similarities to adult psychosis, let us turn our attention briefly to the phenomenon of children's make–believe friends. Imaginary childhood friends (Chapter 9), together with their associated fantasized activities, and even simple daydreaming may all be commonly discouraged by well–meaning parents and mentors. As adults, most of us have broken our bonds to these dimensions—now concealed and distant. Yet these domains surround us and embrace us. Were they truly created in the mind, or are they real? Many argue that they are real and that we have only to relearn their presence. Making contact with the psychic or spiritual realm is not always easy, however. I have been attempting to establish communication for years—unsuccessfully (if you exclude the province of dreams). I suspect that my inability to regain this forfeited gift is a part of my destiny. In other words, it is my strong attachment to this material world that has led me down my current, particular path of research. I believe this role in my life may have been preordained in order to allow me to benefit others who, like myself, are limited by this three–dimensional world. All of us have a purpose in life, even if the purpose lies beyond our present under-standing.

Our senses are our eyes into the three-dimensional world. A select few of us are gifted with the additional faculties of extrasensory percep-tion such as clairvoyance, the ability to view spirits, or other paranor-mal traits. Edgar Cayce's own mother believed that his power of divination was a gift from God. However, in the absence of psychic abilities, I and others like me must use what intelligence and talents we have in this life to uncover the ultimate truths. Science is the vehicle I have employed in this endeavor, and it has served me well.

HIDDEN MATTER

On a daily basis, we interact with what physicists refer to as visible matter. Even the stars and planets that we view in the night skies con-stitute visible matter. However, recent evidence reveals an enormous amount of hidden or dark matter in the universe, which, as its name implies, is invisible to the eye. This hidden matter does not include the invisible states of water vapor or other naturally occurring gases. Nor does it include transparent objects such as glass or water. Rather, physi-cists refer to dark matter as matter that must exist in the universe to explain certain phenomena. Dark matter must exist in the universe if the cosmos is to end in the scenario of the Big Crunch (still controver-sial). Movements of some galaxies can only be explained through the gravitational attraction of supermassive black holes or other forms of dark matter that cannot be detected except by their gravitational influ-ences. Similarly, rotational speeds of stars at the edges of spiral galaxies move at higher velocities than would otherwise be predicted. Only un-seen dark matter could account for these observations. Scientists calcu-late that the current measure of visible matter in the universe (e.g., stars and galaxies) represents only about one percent of the total mass of the universe. If we include black holes and other proven entities, such as neutrinos[11], the percentage rises to approximately ten percent. The irre-futable conclusion is that the vast majority of our universe is veiled and entirely unknown to us—possibly beyond anything we could imagine. Because of this, the possible candidates that fill this informational void are all hypothetical entities, including monopoles (north and south magnetic poles that have become separated), axions (subatomic particles of low mass and energy), sparticles (predicted by supersymmetry), WIMPs (weakly interacting massive particles), heavy neutrinos, quark nuggets, little black holes, and MACHOs (massive compact halo objects), to name a few. Time and scientific research will eventually shorten the length of this list and add to our understanding of the unknown universe.

In the next chapter, we will examine one of the most incredible phenomena dealing with the hidden dimensions—the clairvoyance of Edgar Cayce.

3

The Edgar Cayce Readings

*I*f we accept that there exists a scientific basis for clairvoyance, as one of the concealed dimensions, we then have to ask if the content of even notable, accepted psychic readings is valid. Certainly, the readings of Edgar Cayce are the most remarkable and best documented of any in history. He cannot be criticized as a con or scam artist. Cayce had only an eighth grade education and yet prescribed state-of-the-art medical therapies that were sometimes quite advanced. He utilized medical terminology appropriately and in proper context. Yet he was often destitute. Cayce was usually the first to question the validity and rationale of his own readings. He did not understand them or the inherent unfamiliar medical vocabulary, and he often questioned if the readings were the work of the devil. He prayed and read the Bible constantly. He so doubted the reliability of his own readings that he sometimes failed to utilize them except as a last resort, even when the health of his own family was involved. There are countless stories of last-minute readings for family members when all attempts through traditional medicine had failed, or unwanted surgery was the only remaining option. A familiar scenario would be Cayce giving a reading and prescribing an unknown or unconventional treatment. Cautiously, the treatment would be applied, and, often surprisingly, the patient would improve. This occurred in cases involving Cayce's wife, Gertrude (on two different occasions), Cayce's son Hugh Lynn, and even Cayce himself. In each instance, Cayce was as amazed as were the social and medical communities that witnessed the healings.

THE SOURCE PRESCRIPTIONS

In an extensive review of Cayce's medical and alternative medicine therapies, I found that the medical community, at the time, did not support many of his therapies. Concomitantly, I also noted little to prove his recommendations harmful, possibly because of their low or benign dosages. Cayce and his medium of knowledge, referred to as the Source, were insightful enough to recommend that many of the therapies be administered under the supervision of a medical doctor. Such recommendations were often delayed, since finding a physician to prescribe and support the necessary medication or treatment often proved a major obstacle. No doubt, this led many recommendations to involve osteopathic therapy and manipulations instead of the more traditional, allopathic medical treatments. I also remind the reader that, at the time his readings took place, many of the now outdated medical treatments were widely accepted. Only since the development of safer, more costly drugs, have these older therapies been replaced. I cannot deny that most medical doctors currently view most of his readings with skepticism, particularly those recommending colored lights, the violet ray, ultraviolet light, the radio–active appliance, or wet cell appliance applications. However, allopathic medicine is undergoing rapid change. The number of diseases for which modern medicine now prescribes light therapy has expanded at a swift pace. As we shall see, Edgar Cayce was far ahead of his time.

My research has revealed that the Cayce therapies were supported medically and were credible for that era. Let's review some of these readings and their therapeutic recommendations in alphabetical order. Reading references are noted[12]:

1. **Arsenic**[13] prescribed for acne (1709-2), boils (0078-2), and anemia (1360-1). In the modern era of medicine, arsenic use is limited to the treatment of certain forms of African trypanosomiasis (the protozoan infection which can cause sleeping sickness). Arsenicals act either by inhibiting essential cellular enzymes or by preventing the formation of adenosine triphosphate (ATP), an indispensable cellular catalyst:

> We would begin with taking internally small doses, in the manner as we will indicate, of Fowler's Solution of Arsenic. This is poison! but if it will be taken as indicated, it will purify or cleanse the skin, see? and set the circulation for a general condition . . .   1709-2

2. **Atropine** to alleviate secretions. Atropine, related to belladonna (below), competes with a chemical (neurotransmitter) necessary for secretory activity:

> We would, not hypodermically, but taken internally— take very minute quantities of atropine, see? one hundred twentieth of a grain, taken in the system. *Not* hypodermically, but that it may act through the lacteal activities of the body; for its active *principle* is to stop secretions in the system. Taken hypodermically, it would act directly with those of the head, face and nose. Taken *internally*, in the small amounts, will act directly with the *glands* that *produce* the serums or the fluids for system.   140-31

3. **Belladonna** for stomach spasms (538-67) or ulcers (4148-1). The belladonna class of drugs compete with a chemical (neurotransmitter) necessary for stomach and intestinal activity:

> We find that small quantities of Belladonna, but necessarily administered under the supervision of a physician, will tend to reduce that spasmodic reaction in the cardiac plexus of the upper stomach.   538-67

4. **Calomel**[14] (mercurous chloride) as a cathartic. In toxic doses, calomel inactivates essential cellular enzymes:

Every other day, for at least three to five days, there should be given a cathartic as of calomel, colocynth and rhubarb, [CRC tablets] that the eliminations may be kept at an extraordinary reaction in the whole hepatic circulation.
349-11

5. Camphor for diarrhea (4714–1) or colitis (3776–7). There exist numerous medical compounds that include camphor and/or the camphor name. These "camphor" preparations have a multitude of uses, including external uses for itching and/or antisepsis, and, internally, for diarrhea:

One that is destined to suffer with that condition in early childhood known as the summer complaints, or that of the looseness to the intestinal tract, to detraction of the physical body, unless warned against same. With this, use those properties as would be found in herbs of alum root, camphor and such natures—alcohol mixed with same.
4714-1

6. Cascara as a laxative. Cascara is an accepted stimulant laxative:

. . . Senna, Cascara and others, for stimulation of eliminations.
900-390

7. Charcoal for intestinal gas (5545–1) or "digestion" (4212–2). Charcoal has long been recognized as a simple, safe general antidote:

. . . also taking those Charcoal Tablets for the intestinal system as has been given, that we may absorb much of the toxins and be eliminated through the proper channels.
3776-5

8. Chloroform as a cough syrup ingredient (25–6). Chloroform is a known central nervous system depressant—that is, it depresses the cough reflex:

To 4 ounces of Distilled Water add 2 ounces of Strained Honey. Let this come to a boil. Skim off the refuse. Then when this is not entirely cold but some cooler, to be sure,

add 1½ ounces of Grain Alcohol. To this as the carrier,
then, add—in the order named:

Syrup of Horehound	½ ounce,
Syrup of Rhubarb	¼ ounce,
Glycerine	10 minins,
Chloroform	5 minins.

Shake the solution well before the dose is taken, which
would be a teaspoonful—that may be taken every hour,
but take *only* when the irritation in the throat is severe, or
the cough.   1364-1

9. Codeine for bronchitis (265-12), cancer pain (325-66). Codeine is
an opioid derivative, capable of multiple effects including cough inhibition and pain relief:

Codeine as the stimulant and as a preventative for pain for
the body is the best in the present conditions.   325-66

10. Digitalis for heart failure (0304-49). Digitalis (from the foxglove
plant) is a member of the cardiac glycoside class of drugs. These agents
improve heart function by increasing the availability of calcium to cardiac muscle tissue:

. . . the stimuli *for* the heart's action in that of mild or
minute doses of Digital, or Digitalis.   287-8

11. Dilantin® for epilepsy. Dilantin, or phenytoin, is an accepted
anti-convulsant medication:

(Q) Would Phenobarbital, 1/2 grain dose twice daily,
enhance the value of Dilantin now being given 3 times
daily?
(A) [Cayce] Dilantin as we find will gradually become
necessary to the body, and the use of the other product
gradually increased to the half grain twice daily would be
beneficial with the Dilantin.   543-28

12. Fleet® Phospho-soda® to enhance bowel movements. The
phosphate salts are recognized saline laxatives, acting through their
osmotic characteristics:

The next morning, Sunday, before arising, take at least *two ounces* of citrocarbonate (Fleet's Phospho-Soda)—that is, the salts as found in same. Take at least an ounce and a half to two ounces in a glass of water. Lie upon the right side, with a pillow under the body at the liver area—until this has acted well. Of course, the other properties will have acted before—but lie on the right side, with the pillow under the liver, until the Phospho has acted, see? for this will *flush* the system. Take it in *warm* water, you see.

1693-1

13. Hyoscine (scopolamine) as an antispasmodic. This belladonna derivative competes with a chemical (neurotransmitter) necessary for stomach and intestinal activity, thereby slowing activity:

The natural inclination from a hypnotic (which Hyoscine is) is to slow up the activities of the intestinal tract. [Explanatory note from Cayce to patient, following reading] 5640-2 Reports

14. Heroin for a dying patient. Heroin is an opioid narcotic, capable of multiple effects including pain relief:

Now, we find the conditions are beyond repair in the present experience. There may be only that given as will give ease to the body in the present conditions. Not changing any as is applied, but will the hypnotic be changed to that of one minim Eucalyptol, one minim Rectified Oil of Turp, one-eightieth grain Heroin—this in capsule—will be found will ease the body the more.

4407-1

15. Iodine[15] (Atomidine) "to purify the glands and to stimulate the activity through the thyroid." The most common cause of hypothyroidism throughout the world is iodine deficiency. Nutritionists recommend a daily intake of 150 micrograms of iodine for adults. The normal diet, supplemented with iodized salt, generally provides for this minimum requirement:

Also we would give internally one drop of Atomidine in half a glass of water each morning before any meal is taken, for five days; then leave off for ten days, then give again for five days. This is to purify the glands and to stimulate the activity through the thyroid as associated with the glands of the liver, spleen and kidneys. 1123-3

16. Ipecac as an expectorant. Recommended with horehound (an expectorant) and apple brandy in multiple readings, the addition of ipecac, a known local irritant and emetic, presumably augmented the effects of these other agents:

As an expectorant and a healer for the lungs, and for the cold, we would prepare this: To a tablespoonful of Strained Honey add three tablespoonsful of Water. Let this come almost to a boil, sufficient to take out all of the impurities. Skim off then that which rises to the top. Then when this has cooled—not entirely cold but when cooled—add to this, as the carrier, two ounces of Pure Apple Brandy. Then add these other ingredients in the order as named:
Syrup of Horehound ½ ounce,
Compound Tincture of Benzoin 45 minims (or drops),
Syrup of Ipecac 20 minims.
243-31

17. Iron for anemia. The daily human requirements for elemental iron (typically in the form of ferrous salts) vary between 1—1.4 mg (adult male and menstruating female, respectively) to as much as 6 mg in the pregnant female. Iron is a vital component of not only hemoglobin but also myoglobin and numerous other essential enzymes[16]:

For the blood we will have Iron and Calcium. These should tone the whole system, get it in better condition.
4332-1

18. Jerusalem artichoke for diabetes. Jerusalem artichoke is a source of natural inulin (not insulin[17]). However, as an indigestible polysaccharide, inulin may be utilized as a dietary aid for those with diabetes. In addition, this plant tuber harbors bifidobacteria, beneficial for ridding the colon of certain pathologic organisms (including Candida sp.—a yeast). Note: In Sugrue's *The Story of Edgar Cayce: There Is a River* (p. 227), Jerusalem artichoke is incorrectly referred to as natural source of insulin:

We find that a better balance will also be created by the addition of the Jerusalem artichoke to the diet about once each week (not oftener). Take one about the size of a hen egg or the like—eating it raw. Wash it thoroughly and eat raw, but *with* the meal. Keep these crisp by keeping in the ground, and *not* attempting to keep in a crisper or ice box. (When they are taken only once a week, always eat them raw.) There is a greater assimilation of insulin [sic, should be inulin] from this than from *any* other character of vegetable, and the energies from this will be particularly helpful for this body—because of the disturbances in the pancreas and the kidneys.   1837-2

Of additional interest, despite Gladys Davis' unfamiliarity with the distinction between insulin and inulin, she registered her confusion in reading 4020–1. In this citation, she documented her uncertainty in brackets and reaffirmed the continued veracity of the Source:

Occasionally about twice a month, have the Jerusalem artichoke in the diet . . . This carries sufficient insulin [inulin?][18] to correct the diabetic tendencies or the improper assimilation of sugars, so that these should be eliminated in the greater part from the diet (sugars).
                                                      4020-1

19. **Magnesia, citrate of**, as a cathartic. Magnesium sulfate, magnesium hydroxide, and magnesium citrate are accepted saline laxatives, acting via their osmotic properties:

Also take a cathartic to clear the system of the poisons from the cold and congestion. Taking the Citrate of Magnesia would be the better for a quick activity, you see.   303-9

20. **Morphine** for the cough associated with infectious tuberculosis. Morphine is an opioid narcotic, capable of multiple effects, including cough suppression:

As we find, the infectious forces through the tubercular condition in the lung and the effect at present upon the liver and the heart, with kidneys, are the greater disturbances to be reckoned with. The fluid indicated in the left lung need not be drawn off—won't be much use for it unless other things change, at least. As we find, here it would be well to have administered, in a capsule these liquids:

Oil of Eucalyptus	1 minim,
Compound Tincture of Benzoin	2 minims,
Morphine	1/80 grain.

3625-1

21. Narcotic and hypnotic medications (general classification) for cancer patients. These classes of palliative medications are utilized extensively in terminally ill patients:

Conditions are grave—and serious. As we find, only the administration of narcotics, or hypnotics, is indicated; and we would increase especially the hypnotic—such as Luminal or the like; but, to be sure, under the direction of the physician.   569-28

22. Nitroglycerin for the heart and circulation (1795-1). This inexpensive and rapidly acting vasodilator is effective in angina and congestive heart failure:

Should these dizzy expressions appear, we will find that a very minute amount of the nitro-glycerine—given under the supervision of a physician only—would be preventative of the shortness of breath, the dizziness and fullness of the circulation or the tendency for the flooding of the internal circulation or deeper circulation.   862-1

23. Paregoric for colitis (3776-9) or nausea (3776-7). Paregoric is a compound preparation containing opium and camphor. The opium component acts to diminish gastric and intestinal activity:

(Q) How much should be given at a dose?
(A) Small doses. Half a teaspoonful to level teaspoonful in glass of water, with five to six drops of camphor, with two to three drops—one drop of laudanum, or two to three drops of paregoric. Third to fifth dose, one drop added to this of the turpentine. Lime water, spoonful at time, every

few minutes, or fifteen to twenty minutes apart, to reduce
the nausea.   3776-7

24. Penicillin for urinary tract infection. The penicillin class of anti-
biotics acts to kill susceptible bacteria through interference of bacterial
cell wall synthesis, with subsequent cellular destruction:

> Should temperature persist it may be necessary to give the
> penicillin. Do not give until conferring with, and advice
> from the one conducting the operative measures. 264-60

25. Phenobarbital for seizures (see 543–28, cited above under
Dilantin). In addition to its sedative effects, phenobarbital may effec-
tively inhibit seizure activity.

26. Phenolphthalein as a laxative. Phenolphthalein is an accepted
stimulant laxative:

> (Q) What laxative should be used?
> (A) ... If laxatives *are* to be used, cleanse the colon first—
> then use those laxatives as would be found in those of
> phenolphthalein, or those of any of the *sodas* that react
> with the gastric juices of stomach, rather than those of the
> intestines.   1381-7

27. Psyllium for constipation. Psyllium (Metamucil®) is a widely
used fiber laxative:

> (Q) Could a particular food be mentioned which would
> help this body to overcome constipation?
> (A) As we find, any of those such as figs, raisins, pie plant.
> Occasionally taking the effluvia of the Psyllium is well.
>   811-4

28. Resorcinol (resinol) as an antiseptic. Resorcinol is a known agent
for softening and removing the outermost layer of skin. Its chemical
structure confers its antiseptic properties:

> We would use as an antiseptic, other than the *powder* as has
> been indicated in the stearate with the balsam, preferably

> Resinol Ointment on those portions of the irritations on
> the skin itself, see?   1208-4

29. Senna as a laxative (1561-22; cited also under cascara above).
Senna is an accepted stimulant laxative.

30. Strychnine[19] for intestinal worms. At the chemical level, strychnine blocks the normal *inhibitory* effects of glycine at the location of the nerve synapse. Through this action, strychnine acts to excite the nervous system, ultimately producing paralysis and death through unopposed contraction of the muscles. It has been used in the past as a medical stimulant and tonic:

> [T]his condition produced too much in the system of the fluids from mucous as the lining of the body and crated [created?] by the action of intestinal thread worms in the large intestines . . . To relieve or bring about the normal condition of this system we would treat or give through this system that which will overcome these conditions.
> A tea made from what is called or known as ragweeds . . . This is to cleanse the present condition of this body. After this has been taken five days take as a dose, senna, two grains, licorice, one grain, strychnine one-one hundred twentieth grain. This will be taken in capsule or powder form, preferable in capsule, once a day. 4433-1

31. Ultraviolet light for multiple purposes including pulmonary infections, i.e., tuberculosis. UV light may kill bacteria by way of its direct, destructive effect on the organisms' organic, molecular bonds. It is also appreciated that when UV light interacts with oxygen, the resultant product is ozone, a known antiseptic and disinfectant:

> [Fill] the whole lung area with fresh, pure air, or that which is through these periods filled with ozone of the ultra-violet light or rays.   1548-5

The reader will recognize arsenic, mercury, and strychnine as poisons. I need to make several observations at this point. First, at the time of the readings, all these ingredients were accepted medicinal ingredients, and they have subsequently become obsolete only because safer replacements now exist. Second, recent scientific discoveries have renewed credibility in an antiquated concept known as *hormesis*. This theory, revived recently in the journal *Science*,[20] states that certain poisons or even radiation at low doses can actually be good for you. Examples of poisons cited in the article are multiple, including dioxin, arsenic, and mercury. One researcher found thousands of articles in a past scientific literature review to support this theory. If future studies continue to uphold this conclusion, hormesis may provide additional support to many of the Source's medical recommendations.

Cayce was well aware of the potential toxicity of several of the noxious substances he advocated. He characteristically cautioned the user of their toxicity if the directions were not followed precisely (see above selections for arsenic and calomel). Thus, from an observer's standpoint, Cayce was an excellent patient advocate as well as a concerned practitioner. Keep in mind, Cayce dropped out of school at age sixteen, with only an eighth grade education. Granted, he allegedly could memorize books just by sleeping on them, but there is no evidence that Cayce ever slept on medical texts. From a physician's perspective, communication through the Source is the obvious explanation. I know of no other way to explain how someone with such a limited education could use, appropriately, the extensive medical vocabulary that Cayce did.

CAYCE'S MEDICAL TERMINOLOGY

Not only did Cayce display an extensive knowledge of current remedies and medications, but he used medical terminology in an impressive way, even by the standards of a trained medical practitioner. In addition, his understanding and application of the principles of medicine were entirely appropriate. Remember, in Cayce's time, such knowledge would normally have come from extensive reading and medical experience. There is no evidence that Cayce had any such medical exposure. What we see in his readings is the specific and pertinent use of the following medical terminology and principles (with at least one reading reference cited for each example):

1. **Descriptive anatomy of the digestive tract:**
   a. upper digestive system: "esophagus" (2265-1), "cardiac portion of the stomach" [upper stomach] (416-3), "pylorus" [the muscular valve separating the stomach from the duodenum] (1060-1)
   b. small intestine: "mesenteric" [referring to tissue that attaches the intestines to the abdominal wall] (2265-1), "duodenum" [first segment of the small intestines] (882-2), "lower portion of duodenum—or that emptying into the jejunum" (294-190), "Peyer's region" [Peyer's patches are infection-filtering or lymphatic regions of the ileum] (257-7), "lacteals" [intestinal lymphatics] (951-1)
   c. large intestine:
      i. "ascending colon," "caecum" [or cecum, the first portion of the large intestine, into which opens the appendix], "vermiform [wormlike] appendix," (291-1)
      ii. appendix described as a "scavenger to all the influences" (416-3)
   d. "peristaltic movement" [the specific type of contraction of the intestinal muscle] (3040-1)

2. **Respiratory anatomy:**
   a. "larynx" [voicebox], "bronchials" (2265-1)
   b. "epiglottis" [covering over the larynx and trachea], "lungs" (2675-1)
   c. "bronchi and trachea" (1364-1)

3. **Gallbladder pathology:** "crystallization about the gall ducts" (402-1)

4. **Vertebral designations:**
   a. "cervical," (291-1)
   b. "coccyx," "lumbar" (882-2)
   c. "lumbar–sacral area or over the lumbar axis" (4020-1)
   d. "subluxation" [dislocation of the vertebrae] (2019-1)

5. **Circulatory terms:**
   a. "capillary" (2265-1)
   b. "lymph circulation," "hepatic circulation" (291-1)

c. "spleen and hepatic circulation" (402-1)

d. "coagulation," "white blood cells or warrior cells" (882-2)

e. "aorta" (8-2)

6. **Nervous system anatomy:**

a. "sympathetic" [part of the autonomic nervous system] (2265-1)

b. "ganglia" [nerve cell tissue], "plexus" [network of nerves] (882-2)

c. "cervical plexus" [network formed from the cervical nerves] (2675-1)

d. "medulla oblongata" [portion of the brainstem] (2019-1)

7. **Other organs:**

a. "pancreas," "spleen," "kidneys" (291-1)

b. "liver" (1693-1)

c. "adrenals" (951-1)

d. "ovarian and of the Fallopian Tube" (283-1)

8. **Miscellaneous terminology:**

a. "metabolism and katabolism [sic]" [catabolism or destructive chemical reactions], "prenatal" (951-1)

b. "emunctory" [excretory], "peritonitis" [inflammation of the abdominal surface] (852-3)

c. "Eustachian tube under the palate" (2280-2)

d. "false pelvis" [upper pelvis] (283-1)

9. **Description of a pending appendiceal rupture:**

> [The] inflammation as it is at present would produce to the walls of the colon itself a thinning, and the inflammation would so increase that there would be a breaking, or what is known as a rupture . . . We would advise an operation within the next few days.
>
> 4606-1

10. **Advice to a patient that she would not be healed by "bloodless surgery:"**

> (Q) Could Dr. Francis J. Kolar [D.C.] of Wichita, Kansas, heal me with his Bloodless Surgery [for removal of a uterine tumor]?
> (A) [Cayce] No.   264-38

11. Verification that infantile paralysis (polio) is the result of a virus:

> In the physical attributes of the body we find there have been, or are, the after-effects of an exceedingly high temperature, of a virus which makes for taking away of the vital energy of the muscular and nerve forces of the extremities; or polio, as it is sometimes called.
>
> 5348-1

12. Correct anatomic awareness of hepatic (liver) blood flow: "for twice does the blood pass through the liver to once in the heart" (341-31) The liver receives blood through both the portal venous circulation (venous return from the intestines) and from the hepatic artery (from the aorta)—hence, two sources. I found this passage of special medical interest since it reinforced the Source's complex comprehension of human anatomy and physiology.

13. Recommendation (1917) that a patient undergo a transplantation (by the Mayo brothers) of an animal's organ(s) for cancer involvement of the patient's kidney and bladder: The first organ transplant (kidney) was not performed until 1954.

> 1/22/22 Mr. [1868]'s letter: "On or about March 5, 1917, I took a reading from Mr. Cayce on the condition of my father [4971] about which condition EC had no previous information.
> "The reading described the disease with which my father was affected exactly, which was in non-technical terms a cancer. Mr. Cayce made a statement that the bladder, stomach, kidneys were affected and that the only cure would have been an operation by the Mayo Bros. and a substitution of the diseased parts from some living animal. We were unable to convince my mother [242] that this course was practical, so the disease developed rapidly and was fatal within sixty days of the reading . . . "
>
> 4971-1 Reports

14. Recommendation and successful completion of never-before-attempted orthopedic surgery whereby two ends of a

fractured kneecap were nailed together:

"I [Dr. W.H. Ketchum] had never treated a fracture case before, and this fracture had pieces all over the place. So I went down and consulted Cayce. He [lay] down and went to sleep and told me what to do—what to do and how to do it. He said first to put a nail in there and nail it down. Well, I got a picture in my mind of what he was telling me, and then I went down to the blacksmith shop to get the nail. Cayce had said to bore a hole in there (the knee cap) and nail it down. That was rather radical treatment for those times. It just wasn't done. They had used splints but not metal screws up to that time. So after I got the picture in my mind, I went down to the old blacksmith and told him what I wanted. He made a nail like a large roofing nail, with a large head on it, made out of iron. Dr. Anderson and I and the two girl nurses went down there and bored a hole in the knee and nailed it. Then we put the leg in traction, with a pulley at the foot of the bed . . . This was one of my first cases and I wouldn't have taken it on a bet if I had known what it was! Talk about "sweating blood!" The townspeople thought I was just lucky and that was all there was to it; but at the end of about two months that leg was just as solid as can be. Inflammation all gone. That iron nail was still in there— never did take it out—but it was all skinned over and everything was lovely. He took that nail to his grave with him, about 30 years afterward." [Date of surgery—May 31, 1907]   5779-1 Reports

These readings indicate not only a great deal of medical sophistication for the time but also an incredible futuristic vision of medicine. The above reference #5, which describes the appendix as "scavenger to all the influences," is of special interest. During the time of my medical training, the appendix was viewed as an extraneous organ with no known constructive function. Over the last several years, however, the appendix has been recognized as a lymphatic–related organ. One widely accepted surgical reference[21] describes the appendix as an "integral part of the GALT [gut–associated lymphoid tissue]–mediated secretory globulin immune mechanism" (i.e., literally, a bacterial scavenger). Although it is still acknowledged that you can live normally without your appendix, this citation endorses the Source's knowledge base of yet-to-be discovered facts. The other excerpts, especially those dealing with the organ transplant recommendation (#13) and the successful kneecap surgery (#14), speak for themselves. No one will ever convince me that this simple man and his extraordinary gift were not divinely derived.

4

Corroboration of the Readings

*F*or a physician, a medical review of Cayce's readings would not be complete without examining the readings and the resultant outcomes that were later *corroborated* medically or surgically. These select cases should serve to illustrate the accuracy of the Source's acumen. Although the purpose of this section is to illustrate the precision of the Source's diagnoses, I have deliberately included the treatment plans for some conditions of interest. Again, I ask that you keep in mind that Cayce never *physically* examined these patients.

1. On March 19, 1909, a man with a diagnosis of a "nervous [chronic?] appendix" saw the "Psychic Freak," Edgar Cayce, for a reading. As [4135] related the story:

> "[Cayce] laid down and went into one of his usual naps. Now he had been told nothing pertaining to whose case he was to tell about, and as I had tried everything suggested by seven men and no relief, of course I had little faith in anything. But I was willing and anxious to have him try. My friend said, 'Go over

this man carefully, (giving my name). He is here in this room. Tell us what you find.'

"[Cayce: Yes,] we have him here. A little over twenty-eight moons ago this man wrenched his spine, as a result of which we find an impinging on the vertebral end of the nerves at the last dorsal and numbers one and two lumbar vertebrae. We now find pain and irritation at the opposite pole, or in the inguinal region, worse on the right side, through the sympathetics. We also find some irritation of the bladder. As this was caused mechanically it will require mechanical treatment of manipulation to relieve it.

"My wife, upon being told, immediately recalled the time when I wrenched my spine while feeding my horse . . . After three or four mechanical [osteopathic] treatments, my pseudo-appendicitis cleared up entirely, and all soreness localized at the original seat in my spine. After taking a total of nine treatments, or from March 29th until April 21st, all my trouble ceased, and I have not been troubled since." (Communication from a "public address on October 11, 1911 before the American Association for Clinical Research in Boston, Massachusetts" relating to reading 4135-1)

In a November 1962 addendum to this reading, over half a century later, [4135] spoke before a California study group about Edgar Cayce:

"I think he diagnosed [the location of] my appendix some three or four times. He said it was back of the descending colon [known anatomically as *retrocaecal*]. I didn't know it, until years and years later I had all these x-rays. The doctor who operated on me said I was the luckiest boy in the world. He was three hours getting it, it was such a difficult location. If it had ever gone like any other case, I wouldn't be here now. The doctor said if it had been inflamed—as hundreds are—he couldn't have dug it out the way he did. I've still got a whale of a scar. A retrosacral [sic] appendix is one of the most dreaded operations. It's not uncommon, but it has a bad reputation. Cayce was the first one to ever tell me about mine. Of course, he didn't recommend an operation. In his readings, surgery wasn't recommended very often, but sometimes he would—and then it was as if he was determined about it . . . In other words, he would put it right back on the doctors what to do—as if he knew what was in their minds, too. (Attachment to 4135-1)

2. In October 1920, Cayce gave a reading for [4955]. The original reading is not on file at the A.R.E. However, the patient's husband verified the reading in a letter several months later on January 24, 1921:

"This is to certify that Mr. Edgar Cayce gave several psychic readings a few weeks ago in Birmingham in my presence in connection with making diagnosis and outlining courses of treatment for each individual case. One case was that of my wife, [4955], who at the time was in Kentucky about four hundred miles distant. Since the reading was given, Mrs. [4955], after some delay, has had a thorough examination made and found that the generative organs were involved and diseased, just as Mr. Cayce's reading explained. One of the physicians who made the examination told me that Mr. Cayce's diagnosis was very accurate: that his psychic powers in this connection were in evidence and beyond question." 4955-1

3. Between October 1922 and March 1927, Cayce gave several readings for [2675]. The medical history was complex. The patient recalled that "during the summer of 1923 . . . my [medical diagnosis of] 'appendicitis' turned to a case of chronic biliousness in the disclosure of that reading: I was told to take special exercises, cold baths, and a certain powerful vegetable liver tonic. This I did." (Letter of July 26, 1925, reading 2675-1)

In a subsequent letter dated March 15, 1927 (but still referring to the first reading), the patient added the following:

"The leading doctors here in Birmingham said that I had 'chronic appendicitis' and urged an immediate operation. Soon after this, I began to improve [without surgery], and a few months later you gave me the first of these readings. Nothing was said in it about that trouble. I followed the suggestions in it as closely as I could and felt as well for a year or more as one could want to feel. It is the same story with the ones since given, as you know. These suggestions have been so successful in getting me by that I had dismissed all thought of appendicitis; indeed, I have doubted several times since that I ever had appendicitis. I do not doubt it now, however; and as soon as my strength will permit, I am going to have that removed for good. It is my belief that this complication has kept the relief resulting from the other applications from being as permanent as it would otherwise have been.

"I am glad that I received the Reading when I did, and glad that I deferred the operation instead of acting then as I was urged to do, because developments of the few following days proved that I was in no shape for it at that time. If this operation is not a complete success, or if I do not feel well afterwards, it might be well to have another reading later to supplement this . . .

"I want to thank you again for your patient personal attention. I hope you are feeling well yourself. With best wishes, I am Your friend, [2675]." (Letter filed with 2675-7)

On August 24, 1925, the patient had his second reading. The Source identified this problem as residing in "the emunctories," or excretory organs:

[The] excretory system of the body, and the effects of the affectations in the right portion of the abdomen and the liver[,] show how these conditions are manifesting themselves in physical forces of body." [Note: excretory organs would include the intestines, including the colon.]

2675-2

In another reading two years later on March 9, 1927, Cayce observed:

We find conditions are somewhat exaggerated from those as we have had here before, and that the inflammation and uneasy condition as has been experienced by the body is sufficient to warrant the action as may be taken through the performing of operation to relieve condition existent in the region of appendix.   2675-7

Again, observe that the Source stated, "condition existent in the *region* of appendix," not the appendix itself.

The corroborating diagnosis, at the time of surgery, was revealed in a letter of May 11, 1927:

"Dr. Cunningham Wilson, who did my work, thought that, whereas I had been having so much intestinal trouble with symptoms so complex and confusing, it would be better to make a general survey of conditions there by way of a large incision instead of performing an operation for appendix only. This decision proved fortunate. Contrary to my [expectation], the appendix was not seriously affected, though of course he removed it as a precaution against future trouble. The major cause was higher up, at the right curve of the colon, where ascending joins the transverse [colon]. At this point the colon was dislocated, having draped and doubled back on itself forming several adhesions which made almost a total obstruction." (Attachment to 2675-7)

The final diagnosis of a colonic (excretory) obstruction in the right abdomen conformed completely to the Source's analysis.

4. On July 4, 1927, [283] requested a reading to answer whether she could avoid surgery for a presumed ovarian cyst. The Source's observations follow:

In the false pelvis, as is given, we find the seat of the trouble. In times back we find there was congestion caused in and about the body, when the menses showed there was a congestion in same. Neuralgia, as is termed, resulted from same. Hence there became involved in the ovarian or in the Fallopian Tube, that of a congested condition which has continued to enlarge. Hence we have rather that of enlarged ovarian and of the Fallopian Tube than of a condition wherein there is seen the necessity of removal. This may become so, yet—were those conditions as applied to the body overcome by the application of that that would reduce these conditions and eliminate same from the system—this would not be necessary, and would bring better conditions for the body.   283-1

Cayce outlined his recommendations, consisting of olive oil and myrrh massages, heat applications, castor oil hot packs, turpentine and lard hot packs, exercise, medicated douches, and the violet ray appliance. In a follow-up letter of April 1930, the patient reports that she eventually required a hysterectomy:

"The writings by Edgar Cayce for me in July and November, 1927, were followed carefully with some very good results. The June 1928 one did not seem to do me as much good . . . I will add that with my trouble it became necessary to have an operation through which I came very successfully last year in January." (Attachment to 283-3)

A subsequent letter from November 1960 offered a possible reason for the failure of Cayce's medical prescriptions:

"His [EC's] recommendation of using the 'cathode ray' was so in advance of the time (1928) that I could find no one here in Boston to find it, and all I could get was some violet-ray treatment which did not help, and I had to have a hysterectomy." (Attachment to 283-3)

In summary, however, the Source reaffirmed its insight with the diagnosis of the pelvic anomalies.

5. In a reading from March 26, 1928, Cayce examined the body of patient [348], having received a request from his wife. She pleaded, "I feel like [348] needs something as soon as possible . . . What causes attacks of indigestion? Continuous looseness of the bowels
. . . Is there anything in the diet that should be eliminated or added?"
From the inspection, Cayce observed:

. . . an over-acidity . . . existent in the pyloric, as well as cardiac end of stomach—*one* in the lower end, or pyloric end, of laceration. In the upper or cardiac end, rather that of ulceration. These are, as yet, not *over* large in area; yet unless the condition is corrected we would have the ulceration extending, and possibly *closing* the orifice of stomach proper.   348-1

I am again struck with the Source's flawless grasp of human anatomy and pathology. For this condition, Cayce recommended osteopathic spinal manipulation, changes in diet, use of the Double X Radium Appliance, elm bark, yellow saffron tea, and avoidance of alcohol (except some wine in moderation).
Follow–up readings indicated improvement in the illness until Sep–

tember 1930, when the patient sought employment in New York due to concerns of losing his job. From a report dated September 25, 1930, we learn that [348] underwent unexpected surgery—his condition apparently exacerbated by the stress. The surgical diagnosis: "Ruptured ulcer of duodenum." (348-8)

6. On November 18, 1929, [433] requested a follow-up reading for "obesity, gastritis, [and] menstrual trouble."

In his meditative state, Cayce observed:

> Conditions in *many* ways are improved. There are still some disturbances in the organs of the system, especially in pelvis, that would *benefit* the body were the proper corrections made as has been outlined, and the acidity in the system would be materially reduced—and this condition as is seen in the lymphatic circulation *eliminated* or alleviated from the system by the correction *of* that *producing* the distresses in the system.   433-3

Attached to a subsequent reading on November 30, 1931, a letter from her doctor, dated June 17, 1931, indicated, "She came in to have me examine her abdomen . . . I am of the opinion that she does not have fibroma [benign tumor of the uterus] but may have a fat accumulation or a very congested uterus. I hope to be able to promote absorption of it by osteopathic treatment." (Attachment to 433-4)

As a physician, I am quite aware of the fact that doctors do not always agree on either diagnoses or treatments. The Source, however, got it right. Although Cayce did not specify the exact condition (which was not identified in the doctors' reports), he did narrow the location and problem correctly to the pelvis, possibly involving the lymphatic drainage to that area.

7. On October 20, 1930, [1005] notified Cayce of a diagnosis of appendicitis for which doctors wished to operate. A reading was taken the same day:

> This [body] we have had before [this was the 7th reading]. Now, there are changes in the physical forces of the body since last we had same. In the changes as have been

wrought through the circulatory system, those glands and
those tendons as govern the ileum plexus—or in the
region of the vermiform appendix—we have an impaction
that causes the disorder or distention. This, as we find,
may be removed through the application of exterior forces
in taking into the system small doses—but all that the
system will absorb—of olive oil. We would apply wet
cloths—*hot*—over the area, and then follow same with hot
oil packs, see? first, to open the pores and to relax the
system. Then apply the oil packs—Castor Oil. Following
This, cleanse same with tepid water, and apply equal parts
of aconite and of an opiate—or laudanum—that we may
distort the pain, but do not eat too much—and do not *strain*
the system before this is relieved. *Should* inflammation
arise, or should temperature or extreme *nausea* arise, then
it would become operative. Do as given first . . .

There is *not* inflammation in the appendix. There is in
the caecum, where this impaction occurs.   1005-7

Ten days afterward, the patient related, "impaction removed, free from
pain, normal activity, no operation." (Report from 1005–7)

Although this instance may appear minor, any physician or postoperative patient will testify to the preference of avoiding any unneces-
sary surgery.

8.   On February 26, 1934, the Source made the following diagnosis:

As we find, there are some specific disturbing conditions
in the physical forces of this body. The effects are at times
mistaken for causes; the condition being, as we find, a
thickening of tissue in the muco-membrane activity of the
abdominal area that produces the greater distress for the
body . . . the walls of the abdominal area were pinched by
the thickened tissue in the left portion of the body—near
the descending colon . . . This is not from infections forces;
it is not from any condition that would or could be
removed by operative measures; for the tendency was for
too great a coagulation of tissue at the time of such
measures in the body, and must be absorbed through
natural means. See?   523-1

More than one year later, the patient's wife reported, "Mr. [523] died last August of metastatic carcinoma."

The description of the involved tissues (noted by Cayce) is compatible with either a primary or metastatic abdominal cancer, just as was verified in this patient.

9. On February 21, 1935, the son of [522] requested a reading to determine whether surgery was necessary for a medical diagnosis of gallstones.

In trance, Cayce's inspection of the patient revealed the following:

> There are accumulations in the liver and gall duct area especially, and the poisons from the system generally from toxic forces have contributed to the condition. And if these continue to contribute, unless there are the measures used either to empty the gall duct or to cause the solving, they will necessarily require operative forces to remove same. This, as we find, may be done by the gall duct pump, or they may be solved by the application of heat as from oil—such as the oil packs over the area, for sufficient time to make for the enlarging by relaxing of the duct area itself; making through absorption that necessary, as with a purgative such as from a quantity of the Castor Oil internally—hot; with the properties that would make for the engorging or the expanding of that particular area with the system's activity. Thus we may *empty* the sediments that form there. These are only as sediments, or gravel, as yet; but they produce an irritation and prevent the natural secretions and activities for the digestive system, causing excruciating pain and making for those conditions that are very detrimental to the body.
>
> In either of these ways, or that which would be chosen, we would empty same; which would be *preferable* to operative measures in the present, as we find.   522-6

In a subsequent report two months later, the patient wrote, "Dr. Woodruff . . . has me on Caroid Bile Salts [treatment for gallbladder] and I have been feeling better, so surely hope they are going to help me. I have been taking plenty of oil, so hope I will soon get straightened out." (Letter attached to 522-6)

Of interest, on April 26, 1935, Edgar wrote back to the patient of his own ordeal with gallbladder problems:

"I fought that gall bladder trouble myself for almost a whole year before I got rid of it. I don't know of but one case, [522], that has tried the Castor Oil Packs that hasn't gotten marvelous results. That, you know, is what they used for Mr. [1103]. I have just had a report from a doctor in St. Paul who tried it on a patient in the hospital there with fine results, as well as one in Washington recently. Do hope you make it [all right]. (Attachment to 522-6)

Ensuing correspondence through 1966 noted no further problems with the patient's gallbladder.

10. On September 18, 1935, Edgar Cayce rendered an emergency reading for [1003], who appeared in person for the reading "doubled up with pain in [the] right side [of his abdomen]:"

As we find, there are those conditions in the ascending colon that are in the form not only of an engorgement but in the way of producing—because of the portion—toxic forces to the system . . .
In the present, the inflammation tending towards the caecum area is that to be most mindful of; though with the corrections of the pressure in these areas, and with the adjustments in the lumbar and coccyx area, these conditions should disappear.
We would first, then, begin with the painting of the area over the lower caecum and the ascending colon with three parts of Laudanum to one part of Aconite. Then apply the Castor Oil Packs over same. This should be kept up continually for four or five hours. Then give a soda enema, a colonic—using the high colonic irrigation, as far as may be attained; not to cause too great a quantity at the time, but a tablespoonful of baking soda to each quart of water used . . .
Do not allow temperature to arise. If so, inflammation will have set in sufficiently to necessitate operative forces. However, if these will be followed in the present—with the diet consisting of fruit juices, a little beef juice—and keeping the body quiet, these should—without irritation—relieve these pressures in the body . . .
The condition in the present is *above* the appendix area, and may be seen or felt by the examination of the ascending colon—which lies between the lacteal ducts and the

caecum on the right side, you see.   1003-1

Nearly thirty years later, the patient updated his file, informing Gladys Davis that "he never resorted to surgery and that he never had further trouble in his appendix region." (Report from 1003–1)

11. On January 30, 1936, [920] sent an urgent Western Union telegram to Cayce asking, "When can you give me a reading? Very sick—pain in my right side—is it my appendix [?]"

The resultant reading noted the following:

> As we find in the present, there are rather the effects of an acute condition which arises from a spring—as it were—in the pelvic bone, or pelvic bones. This, as we find, gives rise to the disturbances in the lower pelvis, across on the left side as well as a reflex from an engorgement in the ascending colon . . . [Treatment, as outlined,] should eliminate the disturbances in the colon and the caecum and the appendicial [sic] area.   920-5

Following therapy, a letter from the patient one week later indicated a radical improvement:

> "I am enclosing a check for my reading. Words fail me when I try to tell you how much I appreciate your wonderful help. I have followed the instruction in the reading, and the conditions have almost cleared up. I have been examined by a very fine doctor, and he says I have a chronic appendix and advises me to have it out at once, as I will continue to have these attacks until I do. This does not check with your reading, so I have decided to wait a week and have another reading before I even think of an operation." (Attachment to 920-5)

Of special interest in these records, Edgar writes back (February 3, 1936) to the patient of his own experiences with chronic appendicitis:

> "It might interest you to know that we have had several cases of even chronic appendicitis (according to physicians) which have been corrected without operation. My

wife was one case; while in my own an operation was suggested—even in the reading. [Edgar did undergo successful surgery for a correct self-reading of appendicitis.] Through following suggestions made in her reading, the condition was removed—and she has never had even another attack. That was over twelve years ago. So, I'm sure, even if it IS chronic appendicitis in your case, there are other measures which might be resorted to first— before having the operation." (Attachment to 920-5)

On March 21, 1936, an ensuing letter documented that surgery was eventually required for a correct diagnosis of appendicitis: "Mrs. [920] had successful operation today. Appendix was very bad. She is doing very nicely." (Attachment to 920–6)

12. In May 1936, the Source examined [1167] for complaints of "almost constant fatigue, lack of vitality, acutely sensitive nerves that are very hard to control, intestinal disorders and very severe headaches."
Under trance, Cayce determined the following:

> . . . conditions in the teeth or jaw are of such natures that these *need* to be *locally* removed; for the pressure upon the nerve forces is such as to cause a constant suppression by irritation to the general distribution of energies through the head, the neck and the upper portions of the body. *These* we would have removed by operative forces, yes.
>   1167-1

A letter of June 6, 1936, offered the following corroborative evidence:

> "I have only just returned from the hospital where according to Mr. Cayce's advice in the physical reading, I have had three impacted molars removed. The operation was a wonderful demonstration for, though two large pieces of the jawbone on both sides had to be removed, as well as the impacted teeth (all badly infected with streptococci), I suffered no pain at all. Am still very weak but know that by following all the advice and medication in the readings, I will soon be for the first time in my life unhandicapped by severe ill health." (Letter filed with 1167-1)

13. On December 5, 1936, the husband of [391] requested an emergency reading for his wife: "She is suffering with pains in stomach and back, agony to move, and nausea."

The Source examined the patient:

> As we find, there are acute conditions arising from congestion and infectious forces in the blood supply, and a neuralgic condition—or from congestion and infection there is a neuralgic effect in the organs of the pelvis and in the alimentary canal. These in the alimentary canal become a reflex condition, while the neuralgia and the congestion and infection are through the organs of the pelvis.
> As we find, these may be aided in bringing about relief; but unless there are a great many changes and great precautions taken, there must eventually be operative forces if the body would be saved from a great deal of suffering and a carrier of disturbing forces that would be detrimental to the health of the body and to those about it.
>
> 934-4

Cayce cautioned against a delay in surgery.

From subsequent reports, the husband divulged that medical therapy alone was not sufficient to treat his wife's infection, and an operation had proven necessary:

> "Husband said she had just come out of hospital after a period of observation. Dr. thought she could wait a while for the operation." (12/11/36)
> "She [returned] to the hospital with severe uterus infection. Dr. Waller L. Taylor removed both tubes, one ovary, and her appendix. He said it was a good thing she didn't wait longer for the operation." (Reports from 934-4) (12/20/36)

14. On February 8, 1939, the husband of [1620] pleaded for an "immediate reading since doctors are shaking their heads dubiously, saying her time is short." Additional questions included "Where is center of disturbance, throat, bronchial tubes or lungs? Would an operation avail anything? Is this illness apt to prove fatal?"

Several days later, the clairvoyant, in meditation, offered the following information:

> Now, as we find, this wasting away of tissue keeps the body from gaining; because of the inability of the assimilating forces to recreate or to produce that vital force necessary not only as the combative element in this wasting through the condition which exists in bronchi and part of lungs but this inability for coagulation and for the building of resistance. These as we find arise from those infectious forces which have attacked this portion of the body, from cold, congestion, and then the dreaded conditions [cancer?] as produce this wasting away.
>
> 1818-1

The confirming medical diagnosis, received on March 23, 1939, was "Cancer and tumor of both breasts and a malignant condition in lungs and bronchi." The patient succumbed from her condition on April 5, 1939.

It should be noted that the Source prescribed palliative treatment for this case. However, because the therapy also resembled that given for tuberculosis, family and friends presumed the patient's affliction to be tuberculosis. Although Cayce never mentioned tuberculosis, this case illustrates one possible mechanism through which misinterpretation and dissatisfaction of the readings could arise—all through no fault of the Source.

15. On November 24, 1939, a reading was requested on the condition of [2046], following a traumatic head injury from an automobile accident. Cayce reported:

> This is not a true concussion, yet the concussion exists in those areas that lie between the lower portion of the cerebrospinal system (or nerve centers) and the lower brain itself, or through the medulla oblongata. It is also indicated that there has been an irritation, or a shock, to the lower end of the spine. This produces at periods the feeling of numbness in the extremities. Remove these pressures by the use of heat, and mechanical adjustments (osteopathically).   2046-1

On November 27, 1939, the patient's wife wrote to Cayce, "The re-sult—all [the doctors] agree—the condition is as the reading indicates, but no adjustments can be made until the concussion stops cussing, as they fear to precipitate a hemorrhage in the brain area. Until (as the result of the reading), [1833] was able to suggest the spinal injury as a possibility—they have all been treating him—first for meningitis and then (when that didn't prove itself)—a stroke. From here on we can only hope the reading can be followed." (Addendum to 2046-1)

Several days later, on December 7, the clairvoyant responded to the following question on the same patient:

(Q) What is condition of heart?
(A) This . . . irregularity is the result of the lack of fullness of the circulation through the system . . .

Two years later (April 3, 1942), a report verified this additional diag-nosis "when doctors . . . pronounced that he had angina pectoris [insuf-ficient blood flow to the heart]." (Letter from 2046-2)

16. On April 24, 1940, a father urgently telegraphed Cayce for a read-ing due to a nonspecific eye injury to his baby daughter. In actuality, later communications revealed that the baby had found a sharp can opener and had "thrust it accidentally in her eye." Doctors wished to perform an "immediate operation" for repair and removal of metallic fragments that remained in the eye. Neither the type of eye injury nor the details of the metallic fragments were mentioned in the initial re-quest.

The reading, performed the next day, gave specific and detailed in-structions:

Now, as we find, there should be great precautions taken as to remove entirely the metallic substances which through cohesion there have irritated and still do irritate the eye. While the [retina] is not so disturbed, there should be the use of a heavy magnet for attracting metallic substances. This would be very close to the eye; yet not touching the eyeball, of course; and should remove such substances by capillary attraction because of the closeness. It should even remove the tendencies for the *folding* of the area of the eye itself. Use a *heavy* magnet close to the eye and *not* touching the eye, but so that there is an attraction—and especially of the optic itself—from the vibrations of the body. This would be better than operative measures, as we find. However, if there is the inclination for this to curl, where there was the puncture, then it will be necessary to perform a mechanical operation on same . . .

Of course, from the inflammation produced, this will eventually cause—as we find—a form, or a spot, or a coagulation of the mucous membranes—in the form of a cataract or the like. But we find that this may be dissipated by the use of the applications we will suggest, rather than by operative measures; unless such *becomes* attached at the punctured or irritated surface—and if there will be used these applications indicated we find that this should *not* become folded in such a manner as to cause it to become attached.

The eyes would be kept shaded, of course; and for some little time there would be used the cold applications; also the belladonna and other properties for the dilation and the healing—which would be gradually diminished.

2178-1

The Source verbalized additional instructions for osteopathic manipulations, electrotherapy, and diet.

The astonishing results were catalogued in a follow-up letter, dated May 1, 1940:

"Briefly, almost immediately after the accident to the baby's eye—not knowing how she had hurt herself, we were at the mercy of the diagnoses of the doctors to whom we were sent. Three in number, these men seemed to concur on the one point that an operation was necessary and that there would be a distortion of the pupil of the eye and possibly impairment of sight. After the reading and after Mrs. [1602] had called to learn that the reading disclosed a puncture of the eye, I was fascinated to find that Doctor Erlanger had already discovered the puncture. He was the only doctor to note that fact in his examination and this was before he was aware of the facts shown in the reading . . . We are assured now by Doctor Erlanger that an operation will not be necessary . . . There was a distortion of the pupil—it appeared like the split of a cat's eye. This was caused by a portion of the iris leaking out onto the eyeball through the puncture—the pupil expanded and distorted to fill the gap left by the [prolapse] of the iris . . .

[The mother] called to say that she had just brought the baby home from . . . another treatment and that the baby's reaction today was—for the first time—quite normal in all respects—that she had eaten her first meal without the violent nervous reaction with which she had been suffering the past week. I think I can safely predict complete success for the recovery of the baby in every phase of this injury and its sundry complications." (Letter filed with 2178-1)

This particular case was exceptional because of the extraordinary detail of the diagnosis, not divulged by the solicitation, as well as the medical astuteness and success of the recommended treatment, even by modern-day standards.

17. On October 6, 1942, David Kahn, a long-time friend of Cayce's, phoned for an emergency reading for the son of a business associate, a physician! "The boy has been in the hospital since Sunday, and the doctors don't know what is causing the trouble."

The reading contained the following, remarkable observations:

Yes—these are very serious disturbances; a form of step [strep, or streptococcus, a virulent bacteria], that—unless this is allayed—will attack the brain or nerve cord structure itself [prelude to meningitis?[22]].

In the immediate (and unless something of this nature is done these will develop more serious conditions), we would apply over the abdomen the poultice of crushed grapes [to reduce the fever] . . . Crush and use about an inch [thick] between gauze, applying directly to the body and allowing to remain until the poultice is warm from the body heat—or from the high temperature (for the temperature is at present 103 and more). Then change, making another fresh poultice. Apply these continuously.

2826-1

The recommendations were telegraphed immediately back to Kahn.

Unfortunately, neither Cayce's reading nor the physicians' treatment in the hospital could aid this deadly infection. However, the doctors were amazed at the psychic's ability, as noted from the following phone call from Kahn on October 24, 1942:

> "Didn't have a chance to follow out grape treatment, as he died on Thursday . . . but the doctors were amazed that the reading told what his temperature was at that time—said it was exactly correct for that period. They don't believe now it was the polio . . . They had already given him the sulfa drug in some form, wasn't the right thing for this particular case. He had been sort of paralyzed on right side for a month or so and they thought it was polio, but seems to have been some sort of strep, as reading indicated. (Attachment to 2826-1)

18. From a reading on March 18, 1943, the Source detected the following:

> . . . quite an involvement in the gall duct area [in patient 2434] . . . [the body] is tending to regurgitate [acid] owing to those pressures and impulses from the conditions in the gall duct, rather than the production of too great a quantity [of acid], see?   2434-3

Over a decade later, a June 1953 copy of the patient's autopsy gave conclusive evidence for the findings contained in the reading: "LIVER AND GALLBLADDER: Cholecystitis [inflammation of the gallbladder], chronic, moderate. Cholelithiasis [gallstones] congestion, passive, moderate, liver." (Report from 2434-3)

19. On July 20, 1943, [5057] wrote, "Here is my trouble: Ever since an operation for appendicitis in 1915, I have had the most terrible and persistent dysentery. I have been to dozens of doctors; no one has correctly diagnosed or treated me with any success whatever . . . "

A subsequent letter (August 8, 1943) added, "Since writing you, I have had rather a bitter blow. The medical specialist to whom I was going for diagnosis informed me that there was nothing that could be done for me—that I would be wasting money to go to any more doctors, and that my trouble would become progressively worse." (Letters from 5057-1)

Cayce would not perform the reading until May 6, 1944, nearly a year later. Cayce was also not in good health and would die shortly thereafter on January 3, 1945. The Source examined the patient:

> These as we find arise from a condition that arose from intestinal flu, so that the activity of the lymph circulation through the alimentary canal causes a form of inflammation in the colon and in the lower portion of the jejunum. This inflammation is the source or the cause of the temperature that arises at times.
>
> We find that there is produced gradually a form of anemia and this makes a weakness in the structural portions of the body, as in the feet and limbs especially, and a tiredness through the whole of the abdomen, and soreness across the areas where there is the division in the upper and lower portions of the abdomen.   5057-1

Various treatments were prescribed, including ginseng, ginger, "Essence of Lactated Pepsin," alumroot, dietary changes, and an abdominal, crushed grape pack.

A letter of May 11, 1950, outlined the patient's progress:

> "Condition: 'severe.' Physician's Diagnosis and treatment: 'surgery 3 times, no result. Sporic-intestinal [sporadic?] obstruction' . . . Have, since 1950, had trouble diagnosed as amebiasis and undulant fever. Am being treated and cured at last."

At least one physician, D. H. Fogel, M.D., heart specialist and Cayce researcher, believed that the constellation of findings in this case was consistent with the disease known as ulcerative colitis, which is commonly associated with the patient's observed anemia. Either way, both amoebic dysentery and ulcerative colitis are consistent with the Source's description of "inflammation of the colon."

This reading ends with testimonials from individuals who have suffered from ulcerative colitis and who attest to the success of the Source's colitis treatment, based on this reading.

20. On August 13, 1943, [3160] solicited a reading to determine whether she should undergo surgery for her gallbladder. Surgeons had operated previously in 1941 for the same condition, only to find that the problem arose from adhesions on the gallbladder and liver, not the gallbladder itself. At that time, "The Dr. straightened my intestines, took out the appendix and some adhesions that [were] interfering with my circulation. The operation was successful, and I didn't have any trouble from the operation."

The requested reading for another recurrence revealed the following:

> These, then, are conditions as we find them with this body:
> The blood supply indicates a great amount of toxic forces that are the result of very poor eliminations, caused by the disturbances in the gall duct area and the inactivity of the liver . . .
> The effects produced are nausea, fullness through the area of the duodenum, great quantities at times of gas, especially if certain types of foods are taken—if raw vegetables or raw juices or quantities of fats. These especially cause gas through the duodenum as well as through the rest of the alimentary canal . . .
> As we find there are two courses that may be pursued. One will be rather hard upon the body. Operative forces for the removal of same [i.e., gallbladder] could be quickly done, but there should be real preparation for the body if such measures are chosen. Or there may be the use of hot Castor Oil Packs that may assist in so dissolving the gravel in the gall duct and the gall bladder that it might be drained osteopathically, after a long series. This would require a much longer period but would be a much safer manner. As after effects of an operation, owing to the age and the general conditions that have been the result from reflexes, would be such that it would require a great period of time before the body would fully recover from same.
> The use of the anaesthesia also would be rather the greater shock to this very sensitive body; yet if the body would make up its mind that it would go through with the operation, it might control same.   3160-1

The patient finally opted for surgery, and her letter of December 1,

1943, gave the operative findings:

> "My operation was very successful. But I did not have gravel, as the reading of August 13th said. I had a mass of adhesions around the gall bladder, and the gall bladder was diseased. I had a thickening on the stomach, in the gall duct area as the reading said. The doctor said the adhesions caused the thickening on the stomach, which caused my breath to catch, which was one of the questions I asked in the reading.
>
> "The doctor removed my gall bladder, adhesions, and thickening on my stomach. A week after I was home, I had spasms of the stomach for three days, which the doctor said was caused from the thickening on my stomach, which he had removed. Now this week I am feeling much better and will be all right in a short time. I am so thankful that I wrote you and received the reading when I did, for now I can see I would have been much worse in time. The catching of my breath was getting worse, and I was having pain when it happened. The reading was certainly wonderful, and told just what was the trouble . . . May God bless you with health and strength, to carry on your wonderful work." (Letter filed with 3160-1)

In this case, I wish to point out that the erroneous observation of gravel in the gallbladder was a minor anomaly. All the other associated diagnoses were quite correct, and one cannot rule out the possibility that intermittent gravel might have been, at times, a complicating factor.

21. On March 27, 1944, a Cayce devotee had a reading to determine the source of his problem. Questions he posed to the psychic included the following: "Is my condition curable? Where is the exact location of the trouble? Is it due to a muscular condition or to a spinal injury in the past? Can the condition be corrected without an operation?"

During the reading, Cayce responded:

> The areas of disturbance are the conditions existing in the lumbar-sacral and, at times, in the secondary cardiac or the upper dorsal centers. We would begin immediately having hydrotherapy treatments once each week, includ-

ing the short wave treatment—one time with the application in the upper dorsal and the next time to the lumbar-
sacral area or over the lumbar axis.   4020-1

Several days later, the patient replied to the reading in a letter. He
explained that he had been seen by multiple physicians over the preceding years, without any consistent diagnoses or effective treatments.
He had finally consulted the prestigious Mayo Clinic, where the doctors
verified the Source's analysis:

"Finally, in August I wrote to the Mayo Clinic . . . After
days of re-examining me on my whole clinical history
during my life, again, numerous x-rays and finally a
spino-gram. (This is an X-ray examination in which air is
injected into the spinal cord in order to show pressure
points on the cord.)
"Their diagnosis was that I had a slipped disk. In this
condition, one of the cartilage cushions between the
vertebrae is dislodged and protrudes into the spinal canal
causing pressure on the spinal cord. They told me that
they were certain that this was correct as the spinal fluid
analysis showed definite irritation to the nerve roots.
They were unable to locate the exact place where this
condition existed (in 25% of these cases they are unable
to locate the exact location), so in view of the seriousness
of the operation involved and the possibility of having to
extend the area of the surgery if the first probe didn't
reveal the condition diagnosed, they advised against an
operation at that time. They told me to return to the Clinic
if the condition got worse and that they would then make
one additional test and then operate.
"The final denouement is still in the future. But I have
great faith in your powers and I am sure now that you will
soon be able to record this case as a cure. After the above
history, nobody could deny that your efforts were directly
responsible for any cure." (Report from 4020-1)

Medically, the lumbosacral vertebrae are the most common sites for
a slipped disk. Thus, the Source was again precise in diagnosing this
case.

22. In June 1944, Cayce gave a repeat reading for a patient, [1187]:

> As we find conditions are not good. The blood pressure and the weakening of the arteries, while there is not the breaking as yet, have formed a pressure in the reflexes of brain so that the conditions in the [arteries may] thrombose and the activities of the body cause this general weakness, the inability of the body to rest or to maintain rest when there are those activities of any kind. 1187-14

The prescribed treatments proved efficacious, as noted by a daughter's report years later, dated April 30, 1959:

> "She was active and lived without pain until the last few months of her life, when she was hospitalized and unconscious most of the time. She died on November 12, 1953. The doctors thought she had a brain clot and offered exploratory surgery, but the family didn't want to put her through such suffering without promise of help. She was apparently comfortable—just went to sleep. (Attachment to 1187-14)

23. In February 1952, a mother requested past copies of readings performed on her son.

One reading, from May 11, 1940, noted that the patient's intestines had ruptured into the scrotum (2068-2).

Surgery following the readings (July 1942) had since corroborated the Source's diagnosis of a scrotal hernia. The operation verified "that the caecum had descended through the right inguinal opening and was wrapped around and adherent to the testicle." (2068-2)

The next three cases of corroboration deserve special attention:

24. The extraordinary treatment success of Aimee Dietrich (born January 7, 1897) on December 12, 1902, is reported in reading 2473-1.

Her story begins at age two, when epilepsy struck following "an attack of La Grippe." Over the course of the next four years, the convulsions became worse. The girl suffered as many as twenty seizures a day. Over this period, she saw four different physicians. The numerous and varied treatments administered over this time all proved futile. The last doctor she saw declared her case hopeless and, ultimately, fatal. By this time, the family decided to resort to the aid of a psychic—one Mr. Cayce. Under trance, Cayce diagnosed her condition and outlined a course of treatment. By the eighth day, the first improvement was noted. "[Within] three months she was in perfect health, and is so to this day."

The father reported this testimony in an affidavit taken on October 8, 1910, nearly eight years after the reading.

25. The case of Milton Porter Cayce, Edgar's second son, is of special import since it hi–lights the psychic's own hesitation to utilize the readings, even to aid members of his own family.

Milton Porter Cayce was born March 28, 1911. When the baby developed a sudden illness, however, the Cayces put their trust in the physician community of Hopkinsville. By the time a reading (5784-1) was finally taken, circa May 15, 1911, the Source offered no hope. The infant succumbed to the illness two days later.

26. Cayce gave several readings for his wife, Gertrude, following the death of Milton Porter. Although the initial reading (September 1, 1911) never mentioned tuberculosis per se, the diagnosis is clear from the Source's description:

> [The] body in a state of collapse . . . has allowed this congestion to form in the lung from the air breathed in and bacilli, to set up this condition.

Fortunately, the prescribed treatment proved effective for this condition, and Gertrude would recover. (538-1 through 3)

It is clear from the readings that the Source recommended avoiding surgery whenever possible. As any postoperative patient will tell you, this is not a profound statement. Cayce was well aware of the Source's inclination. From a letter of March 12, 1938, he notes that "out of possibly 50 or more similar cases [of gallbladder attacks, I] have had suggested two operations." (997-2)

There are, in addition to the above medical cases cited, a multitude of corroborated or authenticated readings that are non–medical in nature. Among the many that exist, I present below the ones that impressed me the most:

1. A reading (1916 or 1917) from Selma, Alabama supplies corroborative detail on the whereabouts of a lost sister. Several telegrams sent to the woman by relatives went unanswered. A requested reading indicated that the sister had experienced a horseback riding accident, and a letter would arrive the following day explaining the matter. The confirmatory letter arrived the next day. (4953-1 and 4971-1)

2. Another reading from Selma (January 27, 1918) documents the Source's ability to speak foreign languages—in this case, Italian. This fascinating reading required the immediate help and translation by a local Italian fruit dealer. Needless to say, Edgar Cayce did not know Italian. Even the requesting letter for the reading, also in Italian, required translation from a nearby friend in Tuscaloosa, Alabama. (4591-1)

3. In a reading from April 25, 1934 (531-2), Cayce unexpectedly begins the trance by observing, "[He] has just laid aside his paper he was reading." As might be predicted, the patient indeed reported back three days later, "[The] 'reading' is well done, and for that matter your beginning as to the 'laying aside his paper' is correct." As Cayce devotees are well aware, stories such as this are not unusual.

4. In September 1943, *Coronet Magazine* published an article by Harmon Bro entitled "Miracle Man of Virginia Beach." The article (date unspecified) describes one case of how Cayce, in trance, prescribed "smoke oil" for a patient. A second reading was required to further clarify the unknown substance and where it could be found. After contacting the designated pharmacy, the druggist was unable to identify or locate the ingredient. A third reading became necessary, and this time the Source identified the precise location of the medication on a back shelf in the same drugstore. "Found it" was the subsequent response from the incredulous pharmacist, and the "Oil of Smoke" effected a cure. (294-1)

5. A professor, blind from birth, regained partial vision by applying treatments prescribed by the psychic. What made this reading especially interesting was the Source's explanation for this man's karmic blindness. In a previous incarnation in Persia, the professor had been a member of a barbaric tribe that routinely blinded its enemies:

Before that we find the entity was in the Arabian or
Persian land, as now known, in the "city in the hills and
the plains." There we find the entity came as a dweller
from among the Persian peoples; given to what would be
termed activities of a barbaric nature in its early experience. For the entity brought persecution to those of other
tribes or other beliefs, by the blinding with hot irons.

1861-2

In yet another incarnation, this same instructor had been a Confed-
erate soldier in the Civil War by the name of Barnett Seay. The Source
instructed the professor not only as to the location of the corroborating
public records, but even to the exact page containing his birth record!
The following two passages corroborate the details of these findings:

(Q) Henrico County Clerk says he has no records of
Barney A. Seay. Can you clarify this matter?
(A) We find that they may be found among the records of
the births there.
(Q) In what book and page may the records be found?
(A) In the Births, 557.   1861-13

I did find the record of my birth and also some other Civil
War records in the Virginia State Library, as well as in
Henrico County Court, which happens to be in the county
in which the city of Richmond is located. (Letter filed with
1861-19)

Such affirmations certainly enhance the validity of Cayce's unusual
gift. God's use of Edgar Cayce as one of His invaluable instruments over
the past century establishes that God does intervene selectively in our
earthly lives.

5

Examining the Errors

*D*espite the humility, philanthropy, and altruism associated with this righteous man, I felt compelled to investigate for any possible negative aspects (if any) of Cayce's life or the readings. As I discovered, this assignment would prove difficult. I first elected to review the many readings that were associated with dissatisfied outcomes. To do this, I chose to review all the requests made to the A.R.E. predecessor—that is, the Association of National Investigators (1927—1931)—and the A.R.E. (1931—1945) for membership refunds. I performed this task by doing a content search of all the catalogued readings. Historically, after the formation of the Association of National Investigators, readings could be given only to association *members*. This privilege of membership was an indirect means by which the organization could obtain at least some funding to support the readings. Prior to this time, readings had been available essentially for free (Cayce requested that clients donate what they could, which was often nothing). What I discovered was rather revealing. Of the more than 14,000 catalogued readings, my search uncovered only 35 requests for refunds. The majority (18) were the result of either missed readings, unacceptable dates assigned the members for the time of their readings, or reading cancellations due to Edgar Cayce's illness or subsequent death. Edgar Cayce could not locate the "body" of at least one person (3807-1), not included in the eighteen. That leaves sixteen remaining cases, which we will now examine:

Five people requested refunds, stating that the reading recommendations or treatments were of no benefit to the patient (1313-2, 1524-1, 2271-1, 4328-1, 5080-1).

One patient requested a refund on the grounds that he had not been cured by the treatments (4300-5)—a difficult feat for any medical practitioner.

Another individual (680-1) complained that she had been unable to obtain the necessary "Elliott machine" that was recommended.

One refund request came from a relative who stated that the reading did not arrive until nine days after the patient's death (5156-1).

Three requests stated that the readings did not appear to apply in any way to problems, descriptions, or characteristics of the person involved, suggesting the possibility that the reading was made of the wrong "body" (2023-1, 3136-1) or sent to the wrong patient (3112-1).

One patient protested that the reading never answered the main question that she had submitted as the reason for the reading in the first place (3154-1).

Two recipients were disappointed in their readings—for example, one made reference to the person's former incarnations (2893-1—his "wife did not believe in reincarnation").

Two others either could not afford the treatment required or could not afford the membership dues.

In a further review of the readings, I also uncovered 88 readings listed as possibly "Incorrect?" on the A.R.E.'s own website (http://www.are-cayce.org/readings/readings_login.asp). (Note: The Edgar Cayce readings online are available only to A.R.E. members.) These readings proved quite interesting. Several of these 88 cases appeared to be accurate in their diagnoses, with the individuals expressing apparent satisfaction with the outcome. This left me uncertain as to why they were listed as incorrect. Despite these few inconsistencies, most of these readings listed as incorrect contained erroneous diagnoses, readings on the wrong individuals, or otherwise erroneous information. The errors were as minor as incorrect birth dates (555-1 and 871-1) and as major as a missed diagnosis of empyema (a life–threatening lung infection) in a six–year–old child (1139-1). Once again, allegations were made in additional readings that the psychic had targeted the wrong person or the diagnosis or reading just didn't apply to the right patient. One life reading (1489-1) supplied the correct information, but for the *daughter* rather than the requesting mother. Another reading offered the appropriate diagnoses, but for another person present in the same room as the patient (1422-1). These last two references verify that errors could occur due to improper identification.

A further selection of some of the remaining readings classified as incorrect are presented below:

1. The reading didn't seem to apply to the proper individual: 147-19, 276-9, 882-2, 997-1, 1327-1, 1464-1

2. One or more diagnoses didn't appear to apply to the patient: 113-1, 249-1, 277-1, 882-2, 979-8

3. The recommended treatment wasn't helpful: 751-3, 1055-3

4. The wrong sex was predicted for a forthcoming baby: 199-1 (and 199-2), 1102-3

5. The patient was deceased at the time the reading was performed: 144-1 (days), 333-13 (by 30 minutes), 534-2 (by a day)

Of the hundreds of readings reviewed, I list below one additional example that contains a clear, erroneous diagnosis, corroborated by subsequent surgery:

Preoperative or pre-reading information: None

Reading (January 8, 1943): "We find that the acute conditions arise from an obstruction or a telescoping in a portion of the upper part of jejunum, and this is a complication with a liver and kidney circulation."

Postoperative information supplied *by friend of patient* (January 10, 1943): "The report to me is that the doctors' estimate as to the probable trouble was right, and not the reading: they removed the womb, which was hardened. A bag of 2 3/4 gallons of liquid was around one of the ovaries. The other ovary was all right. The fallopian tube was stretched till it was like a worn-out rubber band. Nothing whatever was discovered wrong with the intestines, liver, or other organs." (2878-1)

There is one further observation that I should include. I noted that there was, in a significant percentage of the Source's diagnoses, a conformity with the presumptive diagnoses asserted in the patients' introductory letters (i.e., requesting the readings). As such, skeptics might question whether the psychic was merely embellishing (as a pre-hypnotic suggestion?) the initial information supplied by the patient, requesting family member, or friend. As one patient observed, "[There was] no knowledge or benefit from the so-called reading. And which in my judgement was merely a repetition of the information that I gave the secretary previous to the reading" (1524-1).

Since the readings can sometimes be rather confusing and vague in their descriptions of problems and conditions of the patient, I can understand such criticisms.

The above citations *appear* to demonstrate, at least for some cases, that the Source did make errors. If the Source truly represented the perfect spirit world, then how could such mistakes occur? Let us examine several plausible explanations:

1. The reading was taken on the wrong patient. Cayce typically requested the precise location for the patient at the exact time the reading would take place. Apparently, the Source required this information so as *not* to examine the wrong individual. There are several examples of the Source being unable "to find the body" for the readings. In addition, some patients requested refunds from the A.R.E. because their respective readings did not appear to apply to them. Certainly, if the Source lacked the required information, I can understand how a case of mistaken identity occurred.

2. The condition(s) present at the time of the reading had resolved by the time of the subsequent medical diagnosis or

operation. Although such an explanation is unlikely for most *acute* surgical conditions, such as acute appendicitis, it is not impossible. However, the diagnosis of *chronic* appendicitis, despite being used frequently in Cayce's day, is a controversial one in the current, modern medical era. Many, if not most, physicians and surgeons will argue that this condition does not exist. Numerous current medical and surgical texts do not even include the diagnosis of chronic appendicitis in the contents. From this standpoint, a majority of today's physicians would contend that most of the Source's erroneous diagnoses of appendicitis would not fall under this category (i.e., a condition that had resolved by the time of surgery).

3. The information source or psychic connection was disturbed. Many paranormal researchers contend that clairvoyants and psychics may not always receive their information directly and clearly from their source(s). They assert that the information might become distorted, the facts misinterpreted, or the connection deteriorated because of other interference. A Dr. Richardson, in a talk before the A.R.E. Congress of 1933, compared psychic connections to that of a "radio reception" (see article appended to reading 360-1). The Source used the same radio analogy in readings 268-67 and -68 when explaining how the channel may sometimes become disordered.

In support of this concept, Cayce interrupted his readings on several occasions due to various channel interferences. The June 1934 reading of 583-8 is one clear example. During this reading, Mildred Davis reports that "the windows began to rattle FURIOUSLY (wind blowing) . . . [The] reading suddenly stopped in the middle of a sentence." After awaking, Cayce noted that he felt "out of sorts." A discussion revealed that the deceased spouse of the patient had been "present and objecting" to the reading. The incomplete reading resumed the following day. Before going into trance, Cayce noted that he was still "not feeling well mentally,—said he understood how one could become possessed." As this second reading was ending, the spirit returned. This time the psychic allowed the deceased husband to deliver a message to his wife, concluding, "for this channel, [Edgar Cayce] thy friend, my friend, will aid thee." Thus, it is apparent that spirit entities could interfere with the channel of communication.

Similarly, in another reading (254-67), the psychic acknowledged the involvement of deceased loved ones and the role of "combative influences" during the communications:

> For, as may be surmised from that given, one that would approach the sources of the [Akashic] information with innate and manifested desire . . . that which is supplied in information should emanate from a loved one in the spiritual realm, and that desire has kept such an entity in the realm of communication, and there are those combative influences in the experience of that entity [the spirit, Cayce, or the patient?] so seeking . . . such contact.

This passage is of added interest since it implies that deceased loved ones were often involved in the conveyance of the Source's information.

Further reinforcing an additional cause of disturbance, Cayce, in another trance (254-67), notes, "[With] the entity now known as [355]: There were, in the field or room at that particular time, feelings in the make-up (which means of the whole body) of those present that made for a deflecting of that being sought." I interpret this to mean that some people present in the same room as the patient had emotions that were, in some way, interfering with Cayce's ability to examine the patient.

4. The attitude of the person requesting the reading played a direct role in the outcome of the reading. "Generally, the best readings and best results came when individuals requested help for themselves or their loved ones with a prayerful attitude or cooperation and hope."[23] This observation, from *The Outer Limits of Edgar Cayce's Power*, is voiced by two who knew the psychic best—his sons.

5. Cayce, from either fatigue, illness, or other complicating factors, misread the information from the Source. Medically, at least, it is recognized that either depression, debilitation, or disease can affect alertness, perception, and cognition.

In reading 144-1, the recent death of close friend Dr. Thomas House probably allowed Cayce's inadvertent reading of the already deceased individual, [144].[24] In a later reading, the Source verifies this supposition by outlining various factors that could negatively affect the psychic:

> Then, that which wavers or hinders or repels or blocks the activity through this channel when in such a state may be from these causes; namely:
>
> The unwillingness of the body-consciousness [Cayce's] to submit to the suggestion as pertaining to information desired at that particular time. Or the activity of the physical [Cayce's?] in such a manner as to require the influence or supervision of the superconsciousness in the body, or ill health, at such a period. Or the mental attitude of those about the body [Cayce's or the patient's?] that are not in accord with the type, class or character of information sought at that particular time. Or there may be the many variations of the combination of these, influencing one to another, as to the type, class or real activity of the entity or soul that seeks the information.   254-67

Although the beginning of this excerpt is evidently referring to Cayce (i.e., "to submit to the suggestion"), it is unclear to which "body" (Cayce's or the patient's) the Source is referring at the end (i.e., "the mental attitude of those about the body"). From the previous references, we know that a multitude of factors could influence the readings. As such, it seems understandable that antagonistic influences about either Cayce or the patient might interfere with the results.

6. The Source fulfilled the reading for the patient's condition but not the patient. When the reading of 534-1 occurred 24 hours following the child's death (from leukemia), a follow-up reading was performed to help explain the error. Surprisingly, the Source announced, "[It's] the condition rather than the body for which this is given—would prove helpful; as a basis that many another body in its own experience might gain the greater experience; if God wills." I suspect this justification was just one of a combination of contributing factors that must surround the condition of a dying child.

7. The identity of the Source was known to vary. It is well accepted that the identity of the Source varied, depending upon the type of reading, the request being made, the parties or circumstances involved, etc. Is it possible that some entities acting as the Source were more reliable or credible than others? Similarly, could some entities more clearly convey or transmit their information through Cayce than could others (e.g., a stronger signal or more comprehensible patterns of thought)? These are all possible explanations. We know that only infrequently did the Source identify itself. Gladys Davis, as Cayce's diligent stenographer, documented the few Sources who did reveal themselves. These included Jesus (254–50), Archangel Michael (262–27 and –28), and the Angel Halaliel (262–56). Although none of these distinguished personalities is suspected of errors, the vast majority of the Source's identities remain unknown.

More commonly, however, the spirit of a loved one who had passed on (previously noted citations) or another closely involved party interceded as the Source. This designated spirit would then act to convey the requested information for the reading. For example, in one reading (3812–2), the spirits of two Union soldiers supplied the answers for finding (unsuccessfully) a lost payroll buried by the Union army.

8. The Source made a diagnostic error. Simply, we must entertain the notion that, on rare occasions, the entity acting as the Source made a mistake. Even if this option accounted for *all* of the erroneous readings, the satisfaction rate still falls within today's medically acceptable standards.

Let us now summarize the apparent inaccuracies of the Source. If, from the total of the approximately 14,306 readings, we subtract the number of dissatisfied customers, we are left with an extraordinary number of satisfied patients. A significant percentage of these have left behind exemplary testimonials to the success of the readings. Critics will still remind us that multiple readings were given for the same individuals, so the true number of persons is undoubtedly much lower. One estimate lists the number at around five thousand distinctly different people.[25] In the opposite vein, however, not all the dissatisfaction was the fault of the Source (e.g., inability to afford the treatments, time conflicts leading to missed readings, etc.). In addition, any physician will recognize that a patient's own subjective diagnosis may not agree with the proven medical diagnosis. All physicians have had cases of patients with only nervous conditions who were convinced they had cancer. Unfortunately, we've all also had cases where the reverse was true—that is, patients who had cancer but refused to accept that diagnosis as a real possibility. In further defense of Cayce, however, many proven medical conditions *may* exist for decades without symptoms, leading to allegations that the readings didn't apply (for example, *some* cases of gallstones, heart disease, adhesions, cystic diseases, even some tumors and cancers, etc.). Hence, like many other quandaries in life, the verdict is still out on reasons to explain all the inconsistencies.

The exact number of inaccurate readings has yet to be determined. Objective analyses would be clearly unattainable. As we have witnessed so far, any figures would have to include the *reviewers'* subjective interpretations of more subjective interpretations (that is, the *individuals'* reports on their own readings). Despite this inherent limitation, Hugh Lynn and Edgar Evans Cayce performed a random sampling of 150 readings of all types to determine a general error rate. Due to their closeness to and knowledge of the psychic, these two individuals were in the best position to judge the results of the readings (albeit, critics will argue bias). Of these 150 cases, 11 of the reading recipients reported unfavorably on their outcomes—a dissatisfaction (or error) rate of about 7%.[26] These negative reports were not detailed but encompassed readings from all the categories of readings, including readings on business, dream interpretation, land deposits, and even buried treasure.

We are left to conclude only that the accuracy and satisfaction rates of the readings do seem too good to be true. The following chapters, however, will furnish further scientific credibility to the Source. We shall turn our focus next to the healing of the body through the stabilization of its energies.

6

The Radio-Active and Wet Cell Appliances

*T*he Source often observed that electrical imbalances in the body could result in various ailments. As such, the rational way to address these problems was through the application of devices to normalize the body's electric field(s). Two such contrivances advocated by Cayce for this purpose were the radio–active (note: this is not the same as *radioactive*) and wet cell appliances. The wet cell apparatus actually generates a small electric current and is believed to act by *contributing* to the body's energy forces. The radio–active device, on the other hand, does not produce any measurable electricity and is intended more to *balance* the body's innate electrical forces.

Following are two not–uncommon readings involving the radio–active and wet cell appliances:

> As we find, while there are disturbances physically we find that these may be best met with the general attitude of the body if there are the body electrical forces applied; that is, with the Radio-Active Appliance. Use this for thirty minutes twice each day, and let those periods be set aside for prayer and medita-

tion. Thus we will bring a better balance to these body forces. The frayed or weary nerve centers will be rejuvenated. The body forces and circulations, where irritations have caused weakness in the limbs, will be much bettered.

Also each evening when ready to retire we would use, for about a minute and a half to two minutes, a gentle massage with a very low vibration of the Violet Ray (hand machine, bulb applicator) [to be discussed later in this chapter]. This will also assist in charging the centers of the body, as the equalizing is accomplished through the Radio-Active Appliance.   3264-1

Also begin with the use of the low Wet Cell Appliance that carries into the system, alternately, Chloride of Gold and Spirits of Camphor; one used one day, the other the next.

The first day, when using the Gold—attach the copper plate to the 4th lumbar, while the large nickel plate, through which the Gold Solution passes vibratorially (in the proportions of one grain Chloride of Gold to each ounce of Distilled Water), would be attached to the umbilical and lacteal duct plexus.

Next day, when using the Camphor—attach the copper plate to the 9th dorsal center, and the nickel plate, through which the Spirits of Camphor Solution passes vibratorially (commercial strength), to the area over the liver duct—which would be about four fingers straight above the area of the umbilical and lacteal duct plexus (and where the Gold attachment has been made).

Let the Appliance be used thirty minutes each day, you see; one day with the Gold, the next day with the Camphor.   2640-1

Wet cell batteries are not new. The automobile battery is an example of a wet cell battery. (Disclaimer: Do not attempt use with a car battery!) The type of wet cell that Edgar Cayce described in his readings is by no means as powerful as a car battery and will typically generate far less electricity than even a flashlight battery. A flashlight battery produces on the order of 1.5 volts of current. Some reports estimate a voltage as low as 20–35 millivolts for Cayce's wet cell.[27] Prices for wet cell appliances, depending upon the model and manufacturer, can currently range from $166 to $300. Likewise, the radio–active appliance (or Radiac®) was selling for $195 in 2003.

In a 1974 letter, Edgar Evans Cayce included the following additional wet cell specifics:

> "It is true that different readings suggested different materials for the solution jar coils, but a general reading on the construction of the devices did not specify any particular type metal for the various solutions. I believe nickel wire was suggested as well as hollow lead wire since they are generally corrosive resistant; probably copper or silver or gold wire would be equally suitable; I don't remember any silver-plated wires or gold-plated wires ever being suggested, but I see no reason not to use them . . . The voltage reading of a wet cell depends upon the difference of the copper and nickel rods in the electro-motive series; this is best measured by a vacuum tube voltmeter and is approximately 1/2 volt, plus or minus. Most of the readings suggested discarding the electrolyte after one month and putting in a fresh charge (the nickel and copper rods were to be sandpapered or cleaned at this time also)." (1800-34)

From a medical standpoint, the benefit to be obtained from the wet cell appliance is unclear. That is not to say, however, that a benefit is not produced. Despite the low voltage generated, caution is recommended in heart patients, especially those with cardiac pacemakers or automatic defibrillators. All in all, I would recommend that anyone considering the use of these apparatuses solicit the advice of his or her personal physician.

To pursue the opinion of the current medical community on the radio–active and wet cell instruments, I executed several online medical searches. I was unable to identify any allopathic medical articles that supported Cayce's radio–active appliance. I observed that even alternative medicine websites and catalogs tend to merely recite excerpts from the Cayce readings as to its use and usefulness. Thus, from a medical standpoint, I can neither support nor refute its efficacy.

In contrast, there exist multiple medical articles dealing with the general scope of electrotherapy. I will outline the various conditions for which electrotherapy has been shown to have a beneficial effect, realizing that the treatments cannot be compared specifically to the wet cell appliance. Each treatment, for each condition, employs different techniques, electric currents, and circumstances. However, for the time being, these studies confirm that electrotherapy has an accepted benefit for the human condition. Whenever possible, I list the appropriate medical terminology used by the medical community to identify the type of electrotherapy, as well as the disease processes for which they are employed. (Note: This list represents only a small sample of the medical literature and is by no means complete. In addition, as with all scientific literature, some of these references will be out of date even by the time of this publication.)

1. It is known that electrical stimulation can strengthen weak muscles. An Austrian study analyzed the various forms of electric current employed to accomplish this benefit.[28]

2. Several studies have demonstrated remarkable anti–tumor effects of electrotherapy. In one article from Slovenia, researchers tested the mechanism by which direct electric currents are known to inhibit tumor growth. Using two fibrosarcoma models, the investigators found that the electric current selectively decreased blood flow to the tumors.[29]

3. In a separate report from Slovenia, investigators applied a direct electric current subcutaneously into the region of two types of cancers in mice: fibrosarcoma and melanoma. This treatment method substantially inhibited tumor growth. The amount of inhibition was directly related to the intensity of the current utilized: 0.6, 1.0, 1.4, or 1.8 milliamperes (mA). The addition of a known chemotherapeutic agent, interleukin–2, brought about "significant tumor growth delay and also [a] higher curability rate."[30]

4. In some diabetics, poor blood flow is known to cause ankle and foot ulcers. Researchers at the University of Pennsylvania discovered that high–voltage, pulsed electric current improved circulation and healing to these diabetic skin lesions. Oxygen measurements of the involved tissues improved from a mean of about 2 (mm Hg, pre-treatment) to 33 (with the electrotherapy).[31]

5. In a review article from the University of Hertfordshire (UK), the

contribution of electrotherapy in the general field of healthcare was explored. The authors concluded the following:

"The means by which a range of different exogenous energy forms can influence the physiologic state of the tissue is well documented . . . The applied energy essentially acts as a trigger that is responsible for stimulating, enhancing or activating particular physiological events, which in turn are utilized to achieve therapeutic benefit . . . Application of various energies in this way can result in significant benefit for the patient."[32]

6. A study from the University of Southern California Medical Center demonstrated a significant   benefit with the use of electrotherapy in treating chronic diabetic peripheral neuropathy (i.e., diabetes-induced pain).   Thirty-six percent of the patients actually became free of pain. Overall, pain decreased in this treatment group by an impressive 66% (+/− 10%).[33]

7. Multiple studies have shown the efficacy of direct electrical stimulation (bone growth stimulators) in the treatment of delayed union (fracture healing) and nonunion of bone.[34] At least one group of orthopedic surgeons reported a success rate of 86% in treating non-united fractures of long bones with this technique.[35]

8. One widely accepted device in current medical practice today for relieving pain is the transcutaneous electrical nerve stimulation (or TENS) unit.[36] This appliance utilizes skin electrodes to deliver the electric current. The current, in turn, acts to arrest pain impulses traveling to the spinal cord. Pain relief occurs during actual operation of the machine and sometimes for an appreciable period following its use.

9. In one unique study from the University of Baghdad, direct electric current stimulation proved to be an effective treatment for cutaneous leishmaniasis (a parasitic protozoan infection of the skin). Researchers exposed the skin lesions to weekly treatments of 10 minutes each. The strength of the current ranged between 5 and 15 mA and less than 40 volts. Ninety-two percent of the lesions cleared completely or showed marked improvement. Sixty-seven percent of the lesions required only one or two sessions for healing. In the control group of (untreated) lesions, none displayed any signs of regression after 6 weeks.[37]

Other widely accepted types of medically recognized electrical modalities also exist but were not mentioned above. These include electroconvulsive (electro–shock) therapy (for certain forms of psychiatric disorders), spinal cord stimulation (a more invasive device than the TENS unit, for chronic pain), heart pacemakers, and cardiac defibrillators.

On the other side of the coin, several studies failed to find evidence to support other forms of electrotherapy or related treatments. These include (1) electrotherapy for hip or knee osteoarthrosis,[38] (2) pulsed high–frequency electromagnetic energy (PHFE) to enhance fracture healing,[39] and (3) electromagnetic therapy for chronic wound healing.[40] Further research is required in these areas.

Another electrical appliance that Cayce advocated was the *violet ray*. Unlike its name suggests, this device utilizes an electric current to produce a static charge—not a beam of light. It is a high–voltage, low-amperage electric source, used principally by hairdressers to stimulate the scalp circulation. It is not inexpensive. One recent catalog listed the cost at $349.95 (December 2003). Like the wet cell, I recommend seeking a physician's advice before employing its use in heart patients and those with cardiac pacemakers or automatic defibrillators.

It is not uncommon that the Source would recommend the use of multiple therapeutic appliances in the same reading. An example from one such reading follows:

> First then, we would take into the system the Animated Ash; one-quarter grain once each day. And three to five minutes after the Ash has been taken . . . apply the violet ray, bulb applicator, for three to five minutes over the lower cervical and upper dorsal [thoracic] area—so we extend from the nerve forces that make for the activity with the upper portion of the circulation . . .
>
> Each day as the body rests we would apply the vibrations from the Radio-Active Appliance, to the opposite extremities, from thirty to sixty minutes. This will make for equalizing the circulation.   782-1

From a scientific standpoint, I can scrutinize, over the course of my career, that medicine is an ever–evolving specialty. Electricity and electromagnetic fields create affects on or in the human body that we have yet to understand. In the province of electrotherapy and electromagnetism, humankind is slowly making headway. Edgar Cayce was decades ahead of his time in this domain. At the very least, no harm is likely with these devices—when used properly and with the restrictions I mentioned.

7

Edgar Cayce on Light

SPIRITUAL LIGHT

*T*he role of light in paranormal experiences, including clairvoyance, cannot be overestimated.

In the near-death experience, Light plays a vital position in welcoming the newly dead. For many, the Light is identified as God; for Christians, Christ; and for nonbelievers, simply as a guide. This presence of the Light is associated with intense feelings of love, warmth, peace, and even knowledge.

From a scientific standpoint, light, like descriptions of God, is ubiquitous. Although in nonvisible form, light pervades even total darkness. Approximately 400 million photons are present in every cubic meter of space throughout our universe.[41] This measurement is consistent with Betty Eadie's observation during her near-death experience:

> "I entered the vastness of space and learned that it was not a void; it was full of love and light—the tangible presence of the spirit of God."[42]

God at the Speed of Light details the scientific experimentation and evidence that supports several profound features of light typically attributable to concepts of God. These include the following:

1. The three *omni's* of Light
    a.   *Omnipresence*: Einstein revealed in his theories of relativity that, for light, time stops—or, in other words, is nonexistent. The ramification of this concept is that photons can theoretically travel the extent of the universe, and time does not elapse. Viewed another way, light waves can be everywhere in the universe at once—or omnipresent.
    b.   *Omniscience*: Any entity, which is omnipresent and exists in the past, present, and future states, shares another comparison to descriptions of God—it is all knowing. Such an entity "sees" everything that has transpired in the past, is occurring now, and will yet come to pass—hence, omniscience.
    c.   *Omnipotence*: From the mathematical standpoint, physicists have found that the above traits cause the energy level of the photon to be infinite. To emphasize this last point, physicists have had to devise a mathematical technique, *renormalization*, to eliminate the infinities of light from energy calculations involving electrons and atoms. Let me explain.

Light is intimately associated with electrons. It is a well-known fact that electrons must absorb light waves to gain the necessary energy to jump to higher electron orbits in atoms (Figure 2). Conversely, electrons must emit light energy to be able to fall to lower electron orbits.

Scientists found that, due to this inherent relationship of light to electrons, an energy calculation of electrons or atoms was not possible without including the energy of light—hence, the infinities or the omnipotence of light.

2. As if these comparisons of light to God were not enough, scientific experiments have even revealed that light displays characteristics of *consciousness*.[43] Briefly, single photons have been found to repeatedly alter their behavior in a manner that can only be explained as specific courses of action that take place retroactively in time! This activity, from the human perspective, appears as the ability of light to predict future events and to alter its behavior accordingly. Some physicists have de-

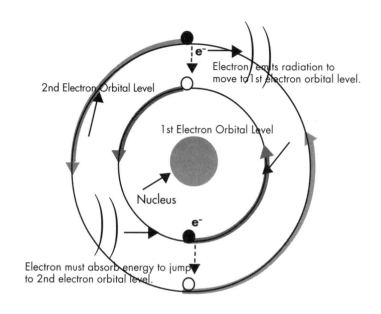

**Figure 2. Electrons emit or absorb electromagnetic radiation
(or photons) as they jump from one atomic
orbital level to another**

scribed this conduct as light's awareness or consciousness of its surroundings.

3. Light represents the loving, guiding entity (God, Christ, or a guide),
which welcomes the newly departed soul in the near–death experience.

4. The last major concept discussed in *God at the Speed of Light* is that
every major religious text in the world describes righteousness and God
in terms of Light. I suggest that these comparisons to a supreme being
are not just metaphorical. Examples of these comparisons appear in the
Apocrypha, the *Kabbalah*, the *Book of Mormon*, the *Koran*, the *Bhagavad Gita*,
and the books of both the Old and New Testaments of the *Bible*:

"Bless the Lord, O my soul!
O Lord my God, thou art very great!
Thou art clothed with honor and majesty,
who coverest thyself with light as with a garment . . . "
Psalms 104:1-2

"The sun shall be no more your light by day,
nor for brightness shall the moon give light to you by
night;
but the Lord will be your everlasting light,
and your God will be your glory.
Your sun shall no more go down,
nor your moon withdraw itself;
for the Lord will be your everlasting light,
and your days of mourning shall be ended."
Isaiah 60:19-20

"Again Jesus spoke to them, saying, 'I am the light of the
world; he who follows me will not walk in darkness, but
will have the light of life.'"
John 8:12

"This is the message we have heard from him and pro-
claim to you, that God is light and in him is no darkness
at all."
I. John 1:5

"For she [wisdom] is a reflection of the everlasting light,
And a spotless mirror of the activity of God."
Apocrypha: The Wisdom of Solomon 7:26 [44]

"The light created by God in the act of Creation
flared from one end of the universe to the other
and was hidden away,
reserved for the righteous in the world that is coming,
as it is written:
'Light is sown for the righteous.'
 . . . Since the first day, the light has never been fully
revealed,
but it is vital to the world,
renewing each day the act of Creation."
Kabbalah, "Creation"[45]

"[Christ] is the light and life of the world; yea, a light that
is endless, that can never be darkened; yea, and also a life

which is endless, that there can be no more death."
Book of Mormon: Mosiah 16:9 [46]

"God is the light of the heavens and the earth. His light
may be compared to a niche that enshrines a lamp, the
lamp within a crystal of star-like brilliance. It is lit from
a blessed olive tree neither eastern nor western. Its very
oil would almost shine forth, though no fire touched it.
Light upon light; God guides to His light whom He will."
Koran 24:35 [47]

"Of a thousand suns in the sky
If suddenly should burst forth
The light, it would be like
Unto the light of that exalted one."
Bhagavad Gita Gita: XI:12 [48]

These comparisons of light to God represent merely an incomplete
sampling for the purposes of this text. They do, however, render a sufficient foundation to allow us to better appreciate the role of light in
Cayce's clairvoyance. What we find (similar to descriptions of near–death
experiences) is that Edgar Cayce gained his information from the Source
after following the Light to the Hall of Records:

"I see myself as a tiny dot out of my physical body, which
lies inert before me. I find myself oppressed by darkness
and there is a feeling of terrific loneliness. Suddenly, I am
conscious of a white beam of light. As this tiny dot, I move
upward following the light, knowing that I must follow
it or be lost. As I move along this path of light, I gradually
become conscious of various levels upon which there is
movement. Upon the first levels there are vague, horrible
shapes, grotesque forms such as one sees in nightmares.
Passing on, there begin to appear on either side mis-
shapen forms of human beings with some part of the body
magnified. Again there is change and I become conscious
of gray-hooded forms moving downward. Gradually,
these become lighter in color. Then the direction changes
and these forms move upward and the color of the robes
grows rapidly lighter. Next, there begin to appear on
either side vague outlines of houses, walls, trees, etc., but
everything is motionless. As I pass on, there is more light
and movement in what appear to be normal cities and

towns. With the growth of movement I become conscious
of sounds, at first indistinct rumblings, then music, laugh-
ter, and singing of birds. There is more and more light, the
colors become very beautiful, and there is the sound of
wonderful music. The houses are left behind, ahead there
is only a blending of sound and color. Quite suddenly I
come upon a hall of records. It is a hall without walls,
without ceiling, but I am conscious of seeing an old man
who hands me a large book, a record of the individual for
whom I seek information." (12-14-33 lecture by Edgar
Cayce; 294-19 Reports)

Light plays multiple roles in the Cayce saga:

1) Cayce followed light to the Akashic Records.
2) The Source prescribed phototherapy in many treatment recommendations.
3) In the readings, the Source also referred to God in terms of light.

One cannot escape the importance of light, whether it is in spirituality, supernatural experiences, or the channeling through Edgar Cayce.
Let us examine some additional passages from the Edgar Cayce readings (referenced in parentheses) that describe God in terms of light:

He is light, all light.   254-68

How hard it be for those that *will* not, when there is being
opened for thee again and again the way thou may
approach that knowledge of the light of thy Maker shining in and through thee in the acts of thine soul, thine
mind, in the deeds that may be done in the body . . . Let
the light, even the light of Him, open thine heart, open
thine mind, that He may Come in. For, He standeth near.
He will direct, He will bring cheer to thee.   378-46

For in Him is the light, and the light is the light of the
world, and it shineth into the dark places; for as an
[example] came that light into the world, that MAN—the
helpmate of God in His creative forces—might give that
reflected light back, in its glorified form.   943-2

So in deeds of men, or in the acts and thoughts, or ideals of man—however they may be made accessible to the mental being—does same make for that which is life, light, understanding. Then it bears the seed and the stamp of divine privilege, divine understanding; for God IS life, light, and immortality.   254-55

"God said, Let there be light, and there was light." This was not an activity from the sun, or light as shed from any radial influence, but it was the ability of consciousness coming into growth from the First Cause. Then, what is the light? Who is the light? These are indicated as sources, the way . . . For there was given to individual souls or entities—as to this entity—the ability to choose, or that light (which is the ability to choose for self)—the WILL; to know self to be one with the whole or the Creative Force, and yet choosing the direction or the spirit, or the purpose, the hope, with which it shall be directed.
                                                      2528-2

Let not thy heart troubled; ye believe in God, believe also in Him—who is able to quicken the life as it flows through thy body, thy mind, thy soul, to a full regeneration in the material world, then hope in the mental, the truth in the spiritual. For, He IS truth, and the light, the way; that each soul may find the way from the darkness back to God—even as He.   2448-2

For the soul seeks growth; as Truth, as Life, as Light, *is* in itself. God *is,* and so is life, light, truth, hope, love. And those that abide in same, grow . . . For, thus does the soul find the relationships to the Maker; whether there is the god of light and love and hope, or that which was separated from same that makes for despair, for night, and for those things that do hinder the approach.   257-123

He sent His Son, that in His life and sacrifice we might get a physical manifestation of *light* through *love.* That as He in His service to His fellow man might show to us God; and that we might also manifest divine attributes.   262-130

Thus the needs for the entity to lean upon the arm of Him who is the law, and the truth and the light . . . As has been indicated for the entity, the Lights that would aid in checking—even in helping the disturbed area in the spine by the use of this high vibration. Electricity or vibration is that same energy, same power, ye call God. Not that God is an electric light or an electric machine, but that vibration that is creative is of that same energy as life itself.

2828-4

The above citations clearly imply a relationship between light and God. In addition, several excerpts suggest alternate associations. For example, 2528-2 indicates a relation with free will and the freedom of choice. Alternately, 2828-4 hints at a connection with the life force itself. From these readings, the Source makes a clear case that the light is not just like "an electric light" (2828) but is an intimate quality or characteristic of our Creator. Recall that entities that travel at light speed can be everywhere in the universe at once, with no restrictions as to past, present, or future. Such entities are capable of witnessing any event in the universe, from any time past or yet to come. As previously discussed, this omnipresence equates to omniscience. If we now include these added Cayce characterizations to light, especially that of free will (i.e., the very act of the decision-making process or thought itself), we can better appreciate the foregoing comparison to consciousness.

From the lecture of December 14, 1933 (reading 294-19, cited earlier), Cayce recalled how, as the trance was initiated, he usually passed through several spirit-filled levels, including those containing "horrible shapes, grotesque forms." During this time, Cayce was always conscious of the Light, which he followed until he arrived at the Hall of Records. During reading 1256-1 (August 26, 1936), however, he remembered how his typical journey to the information source changed. During this particular reading, Cayce reported "going for the akashic records in a different from usual manner, traveling on a blue-purple-silver light, going straight to the house of records without passing through darkness or horrible sights or planes." Even from this report of an altered journey, Cayce reinforced his consistent need to follow the Light—strikingly similar to near-death descriptions.

In 1912, Cayce hinted at his close relationship to the Light in a poem he wrote to his wife, Gertrude:

> "I asked the roses as they grew
> Richer and lovelier in their hue
> What made their buds so rich and bright
> They answered: Looking Toward The Light."

Before we end our contemplations on the relationships between light, God, time, and humankind, it is interesting to note one additional assertion of the Source—one that correlates closely to the postulates of Albert Einstein. In the following text, Cayce divulges that time represents a dimension that exists only for beings of the material world. That is, time does *not* exist for spiritual entities or light:

> What is light, then, in that sense? In that city, in that place, there is no need of the sun, nor of the moon, nor the stars; for He is the *Light;* He *is* Light, and in Him is no darkness at all!
>
> "Let there be light," then, was that consciousness that Time began to be a factor in the experience of those creatures that had entangled themselves in matter; and became what we know as the Influences in a material plane. And the moving force and the life in each, and the activities in each are from the Spirit.
>
> Hence as we see, the divisions were given then for the day, the night; and then man knew that consciousness that made him aware that the morning and the evening were the first day.
>
> What is our experience? Have we visioned, have we understood, have we even attempted to comprehend what is the meaning of the evening and the morning being the first day of an infant entering the material plane? a soul taking on flesh, its attributes, its whole experiences in heaven, in earth, in all the Influences about the earth?
>
> Let us each study same. We will catch a new vision of what Time and Space begin to mean. Then we know that with Patience you mothers have waited and known from this or that experience those awakenings, those awarenesses of the activity; and we see the creation of the world, as the awareness of these influences that have become enmeshed, entangled into matter; that are seeking they know not what. 262-115

Einstein, similar to what the Source verbalized above, taught us that space and time are variables in the universe—not the constants we think them to be. God and light are not restricted by space and time. As humans, however, we are trapped in the material, particulate world of time and space—just as Einstein and Cayce asserted.

HEALING LIGHT

Let us turn our attention now from the spiritual characteristics of light to its physical and healing attributes. Cayce enthusiasts are well acquainted with the readings' advocacy of light in the treatment of specific ailments. One exemplary passage follows:

> (Q) What light should be used?
> (A) [Cayce] Any penetrating light. That of the dry heat, or that that acts the quickest with the blood stream, see? for, as is seen, this is the effect of light—whatever nature that may be applied to a body: All bacilli or all germs are afraid, as it were, of light—or light is destructive to all. Some, as is seen, accumulate in heat that is not penetrating. Hence the variation in the quartz light, the ultraviolet light, the blue light, the red light—each one taking out that that filters through the system. Hence for this, that one most penetrating without being destructive to the tissue proper.   140-21

This selection is interesting from its comment regarding the reaction of germs to light. From a medical standpoint, you cannot make any general remarks about bacteria. Some microbes have adapted so that they are quite resistant to many environmental influences, including heat and light. Some bacteria may exist for years under seemingly inhospitable conditions. On the other hand, it is well known that ultraviolet light kills many common types of disease-producing microorganisms. I believe it is these organisms to which the Source is referring. A secondary effect of light, through the production of heat, plays a separate but equally important role. Any source of warmth, when applied to an area of infection or inflammation, increases circulation. Increased blood flow to an inflamed tissue causes an influx of disease-fighting leukocytes or killer cells, in addition to increased healing through oxygenation. Thus, the effects of light are two–fold, with both direct and indirect bactericidal and healing activities.

The next passage portrays a further dimension into the healing effects of light:

> During that period have applied for a minute to a minute and a half the ultra-violet ray light, (the Mercury Light) with the green glass projected between the light and the body, not more than a minute and a half. Apparently the projection of the green glass deflects the very rays intended to be used by the ultra-violet. True, it does take some rays from the light; yet the penetrating rays that are carried through are deflected or broken sufficiently that the green presents more of a healing power to the conditions where there are those tendencies for inflammation in the mucous membranes or soft tissue, where there is the greater flow of lymph circulation throughout the body— soft tissue of face, lungs, organs of the digestive system, the abdominal area, through the whole alimentary canal. All will be aided and there will be less tendency for the accumulations that may, if there are irritations, become malignant in their nature.   3574-1

Before we dissect the significance of this excerpt, let us examine the historical account of phototherapy. In 1903, Niels Finsen, a Danish physician, won the Nobel Prize for Medicine. This prestigious honor was awarded for Finsen's work on phototherapy, primarily for his research on two diseases—smallpox and lupus vulgaris. Lupus vulgaris is a form of cutaneous tuberculosis, *not* systemic lupus erythematosus as one might have guessed. What Finsen discovered in his investigations were the various qualities inherent in the different frequencies of light.

Visible light (4.3 X 10^{14}–7 X 10^{14} cycles per second) can be broken down into the different colors of the rainbow: red, orange, yellow, green, blue, indigo, and violet. Violet has the highest frequency (hence, the greatest energy), and red, the lowest. Infrared and ultraviolet are spectrums of light that extend into the non–visible range. As the frequencies of light (visible or non–visible) increase, the light energies impart increasingly destructive capabilities. Thus, ultraviolet light, x–rays, and gamma rays are increasingly more damaging to living tissues.

At the opposite end of the light spectrum, we observe that, as the frequencies of light decrease, the ability to generate heat increases. Thus, with decreasing frequencies of light, infrared and microwave radiation are produced, respectively. Below microwave radiation are the TV, short wave, and broadcast radio bands. Electronic oscillators can produce electromagnetic waves as high in frequency as microwaves. However, above this level, the electromagnetic radiation (EMR) must be produced through molecular and atomic oscillations.

It is with this information in mind that we return to the research of Niels Finsen. Dr. Finsen was interested in the healing effects of light. He discovered initially that direct UV light made the lesions of smallpox worse. He then experimented with filtering out the deleterious light rays. Finsen found that red light best accelerated the healing of the smallpox lesions. What we can appreciate now are two things: (1) the red coloration of the glass filtered out the higher frequencies of the visible light spectrum (accentuating the heat–conferring waves), and (2) the glass itself acted as a filter of the destructive UV rays. It is currently appreciated that clear glass alone will block most UV–A light and about half of UV–B light. With one stroke, Dr. Finsen had discovered two benefits of red–colored glass in the treatment of smallpox skin lesions.

When the doctor directed his light research towards the plaques of lupus vulgaris, however, he discovered just the opposite to be true— these lesions responded better to exposure with intense, unfiltered ultraviolet light (with its direct destructive properties). The results were impressive: about 50% of the cases were cured, nearly 45% were partially cured, and the remaining 5% observed no benefit. Thus, one physician used two entirely separate characteristics of light to exploit different healing properties. Dr. Finsen, like the Edgar Cayce readings, showed how the varying attributes and colors of light might be used for the advantage of humankind.

If we re–examine the prior Cayce excerpt (3574-1, repeated in part below), we can now better understand its reference to "deflecting" the unwanted ultraviolet rays:

> During that period have applied for a minute to a minute
> and a half the ultra-violet ray light, (the Mercury Light)
> with the green glass projected between the light and the

body, not more than a minute and a half. Apparently the projection of the green glass deflects the very rays intended to be used by the ultra-violet. True, it does take some rays from the light; yet the penetrating rays that are carried through are deflected or broken sufficiently that the green presents more of a healing power to the conditions where there are those tendencies for inflammation . . .   3574-1

Over the recent decades, therapeutic advances in phototherapy have made their way into the armamentarium of allopathic medicine. This field is progressing rapidly, and I fully recognize that the citations I am presenting may likely be out of date by the time of this publication. Even so, I have no doubt that these future advances will only lend further testimony to the uses of light in the treatment of the human form.

Currently, a plethora of medical information already exists to support the role of light therapies for a wide host of ailments. Let us review some of the current medical literature on light treatments:

1. Prophylactic ultraviolet (UV)-B and psoralen (a light–activated drug) plus UV-A (or PUVA) light therapies are (paradoxically) documented to prevent several light–triggered skin diseases (photodermatoses).[49]

2. Phototherapy is the standard of care for neonatal hyperbilirubinemia ("yellow jaundice of the newborn").

3. UV-B light is standard therapy for psoriasis and atopic dermatitis.

4. PUVA is accepted therapy for cutaneous T-cell lymphoma and vitiligo.

5. Narrowband UV-B phototherapy is an alternative treatment of early mycosis fungoides (a cutaneous T-cell lymphoma).[50]

6. A review article found that UV-A has shown some promising results for localized scleroderma, systemic lupus erythematosus, and other dermatologic conditions.[51]

7. Phototherapy is the standard treatment for seasonal affective disorder, a depressive illness.

8. Researchers found that light exposure plus medication was more effective (improved energy and mood) than medicines alone for some

forms of depression, particularly bipolar affective disorder.[52]

9. Both therapeutic laser and polarized light resulted in beneficial healing of episiotomy wounds.[53]

10. UV–B phototherapy offered benefit to skin lesions in patients with cutaneous graft versus host disease (a potential bone marrow transplant complication) who were already taking high doses of immunosuppressive medications.[54]

11. High–intensity, narrow–band, blue light therapy reduced the number of acne–causing bacteria (*Propionibacterium acnes*, although not *Staphylococcus epidermidis*).[55]

12. Narrowband UV–B light reduced the pruritus (itching) of polycythemia vera (a blood–related illness).[56]

13. One study revealed how phototherapy imparts its immunologic (or disease–fighting) benefits (an improved shift occurs in the number of suppressive lymphocytes).[57]

14. Argon green laser treatment of the eye showed promising results for age–related maculopathy.[58]

15. Laser photocoagulation has offered encouraging results for an expanding host of diseases and tissue abnormalities (e.g., retinal aneurysms,[59] nasal turbinate hypertrophy,[60] telangiectasias, leukoplakia, papillomatoses,[61] Barrett's esophagus,[62] glaucoma, various urological procedures,[63] and a host of vascular and pigmented skin lesions[64]). The treatment of diabetic retinopathy by this modality is one of its most common applications.

16. Photodynamic therapy has emerged as a novel approach for solid and hematologic cancers. This medical technique applies a photosensitive drug that, when exposed to visible light, destroys the malignant tissue.[65]

Researchers have found that the colors, or lack thereof, utilized in these various types of phototherapies impart specific consequences to the recipient tissues, just as Finsen observed. For instance, light from a yellow laser is preferentially absorbed by the oxyhemoglobin component of blood. This characteristic explains its success in the preferential eradication of vascular lesions such as telangiectasia (enlargements of small blood vessels) and port–wine stains (nevi flammeus). Similarly, the selective absorption of blue–green light by the pigment melanin demonstrates the ability of the argon laser to destroy pigmented lesions, e.g., café–au–lait spots and lentigines. The CO2 laser is largely colorless but emits an infrared beam of photons. Intracellular water absorbs this wavelength. Hence, the nonselective nature of this laser explains the wider tissue damage and scarring seen with its use.

The krypton red laser, or any red light, confers the wave frequency necessary to activate the drug porfimer sodium (Photofrin®) in the destruction of cancer cells. The use of photosensitive chemicals like Photofrin to destroy malignant tissue is known as *photodynamic* therapy. Therapists inject this photosensitizing agent into the bloodstream. Although the drug is distributed throughout the body, the rapidly dividing cells present in most cancers retain the chemical for a longer period of time. The target tissue is then exposed to the red light source. The combination of the light and the photochemical catalyzes the resultant, deadly reaction. For cancers of the bladder, lung, throat, or esophagus, a scope is utilized to project the laser light onto the involved tissue. Although a physician will employ the laser treatment within the first two to three days following injection, the patient remains at risk for delayed photosensitivity reactions to the eyes and skin for up to six to eight weeks. Patients must avoid sunlight and other sources of intense light for this time period. A newer photosensitizing agent, known as BPD verteporfin, is triggered by UV–A wavelengths in addition to red light and may be found useful for other conditions.

Although the color and wavelength of light convey most of its healing properties, some confusion still exists in the traditional medical literature. For example, one study found no difference between an argon green laser and a krypton red laser in the treatment of abnormal vessel formation (subfoveal choroidal neovascularization) in age–related macular degeneration (AMD).[66] Another article found no statistical differences between the use of blue, blue–green, or conventional light therapy in the treatment of neonatal hyperbilirubinemia (the common condition of yellow jaundice in the newborn).[67] I have no doubt that the future will shed further insight into the intriguing dynamic of color phototherapy.

Through this past analysis of the characteristics of light, science has offered clarification of the Cayce readings and a better definition of the significant roles of light in our universe and lives—both from the spiritual and physical perspectives.

We have noted how the spiritual traits of light suggest an intimate relationship with God, implying the two may be one and the same. Like God, the Source and its light reside in a realm that is normally concealed from the average individual. For most of us, these dimensions are revealed at only special times—for example, in near-death experiences, dreams, episodes of clairvoyance, or other paranormal encounters including the past-life regressions of hypnotherapy. Obviously, to believe in past-life regressions, you must also believe in reincarnation.

Cayce enthusiasts are well aware that the concept of reincarnation and the life readings go hand-in-hand. Many individuals who received life readings also received news of their previous lives, including their former names and locales. Edgar, as well as his first son, Hugh Lynn, initially struggled over the acceptance of this foreign philosophy. They especially grappled over its conflicts with their Christian heritage, before realizing its compatibilities.

Let us slowly begin to build the case for reincarnation, which we will take up in more detail in the next chapter. Before proceeding to an in-depth discussion of reincarnation, we need to briefly examine the additional role of light in this philosophy.

We have examined the critical role of light in the world's religious texts, the Cayce readings, Einstein's theories of relativity, quantum physics, and other paranormal phenomena including the near-death experience. However, I have left out of the discussion one last, but intriguing, phenomenon involving light—past-life regressions. Light assumes as equally an important role in this form of hypnotherapy as it does in other paranormal events. Hypnotherapists who practice past life regression therapy commonly encounter the element of light.

The two most prevalent light experiences appear under different past-life circumstances. The first is in the form of the typical near-death experience. When individuals relive their former lives, they are also capable of reliving the profound moments of their deaths. During these instances, they also recall the full near-death event—including the warmth, peace, and love associated with the Light. The second light-related event is far less common but all-the-more interesting. During some past-life regressions, the patients may announce that they are reliving past lives in which they have no physical bodies whatsoever. In his *Past Lives, Future Lives*,[68] Dr. Bruce Goldberg describes several such cases. These patients note that they lack human bodies, existing instead as pure energy or, more specifically, light. These entities were not alone. They existed amidst other light beings and communicated telepathically! As quanta of light, these individuals still had existences whereby they learned, taught, and—as certainly as photons—traveled throughout the universe. In one case that Dr. Goldberg regressed, the patient's former light entity was sent "to another planet to monitor the activities of a rapidly evolving culture."[69] Indeed, these spirits continued to learn and live, even as beings of pure energy.

This type of existence is also compatible with many Eastern philosophies and religions. In the *Tibetan Book of the Dead*, or *Bardo Thödol*, the newly dead experience "the Radiance of the Clear Light of Pure Reality. Recognize it . . . Thine own consciousness, shining, void, and inseparable from the Great Body of Radiance, hath no birth, nor death, and is the Immutable Light." [70] Similarly, the Bhagavad Gita (Indian religious text) notes that the goal of humankind is the achievement of nirvana or unity with God, "the Supreme Brahman, the Supreme Station (or Light)."[71]

What we learn is that light plays many different roles on "the other side." To graduate to the light plane(s) is the ultimate goal of humankind. Eastern religions advocate this form of evolution through reincarnation. While we exist and continue to be reincarnated upon the earthly plane, we strive to learn to live as God taught (and as Christ exemplified). In addition, we must pay off our past karmic debts. If we "killed by the sword" in a past life, then we must be killed by the sword in a future life. When our karmic debts are paid and spiritual perfection is achieved, we graduate to the light plane or the level of nirvana. Depending upon the religion or philosophy involved, there may exist other levels or planes through which we have to progress, even after advancing beyond the earth plane. These additional levels may go by the names of planes, spheres, bhuvanas, swargas, etc. The greatest leap, however, appears to be the initial one from the earth plane. This advancement is marked by the abandonment of materialism and the human form in exchange for pure consciousness, spirit, and light. These are the levels in which angels, the Source (and all knowledge), the Light, and, possibly, God reside. I say "possibly" only to suggest that God is everything and infinite. As such, I am not convinced that God can be confined but is probably all things, all levels, and all planes.

God is aware of all things, including our innermost thoughts. This can be a frightening concept were it not for the knowledge of God's unlimited capacity for forgiveness. An additional piece of the forgiveness puzzle will be addressed when we delve more fully into the deliberation over karma and reincarnation. The case for karma and reincarnation will gain added support as we examine evidence for these concepts from no less a source than the *Bible* itself.

8

Reincarnation—The Life Readings

*I*n 1923, upon prompting from an Arthur Lammers of Dayton, Ohio, Edgar Cayce gave his first *life* reading. These readings differed from all the previous *physical* readings in that they dealt primarily with spiritual and philosophical issues. This deviation in practice represented a radical turning point in Cayce's life. The viewpoints expressed by the Source on the issues of theology, astrology, and past lives were hard for even Cayce to accept. The following excerpt (from 490-1) exemplifies these readings:

> What *is* the film that makes between time and space? That's what you are looking for, [490]! You'll find it!
> This film—in this film is the difference between the movement OF the atomic force about its center and the impression that is made *upon* those passing *between* light and heat, not darkness, for darkness may not exist where light has found its way. Though you may not be conscious or aware of its existence, its rays from the very records of time and space turn their emanations to give to a finite mind the dimensions themselves.
> As to the application of self respecting the influ-

ences upon the entity in its sojourns in the earth, we find:

Before this the entity was among those peoples to whom the inventor of the steam's application to the motor, or in France, to whom Fulton went—in the name Eben Claire [?], and the entity was among those that were in this household to whom the entity or body Fulton came; and the entity aided in the material surroundings, but during the sojourn in that experience applied self in attempting to determine ways and means and manners to carry out the ideas that were gathered by the entity Eben in its association with that body Fulton during its sojourn in that experience. Little has been heard, little has been gathered of the entity's activities in that sojourn along the Seine, yet much in the soul development, much in the abilities of the entity in the present in *determination* arises from the experiences in that particular period.

Before this we find the entity was in quite a different, yet quite a close character of development; for he was during those periods when the great artist, the great musician, the great scientist was attempting to make the first experiments with lighter than air machines, or painting the pictures that have become as the mystery of the smile of that particular one.

The entity then, in the name Guiraleldio, was that one who aided DaVinci when much experimentation was made, and much that has been accredited to the scientist DaVinci in the experimentations made may rather have been accredited to this entity during that sojourn.

The entity lost and gained in the experience, for—losing confidence in the correct understandings or relations that were existing in the entity's environs in that experience—the entity wasted much of its ability in riotous living association; yet the abilities, the activities in the inner self, if they are kept with an ideal in the foreground—that is rather of the spiritual than of the material, kept *as* that guiding star, that guiding home; for *ever* should the entity remember, though ye gain the whole world and lose thine own soul it is nothing.

Before this we find the entity was in that land now known as the Egyptian, during those periods when there were the sojournings from the Atlantean land.

The entity then was among the peoples that were of *one* in Atlantis, that journeyed to Egypt and aided in those establishments of the experimentations that dealt with the principles of plant and animal, rather than mineral, as to the applications of these principles to the curative forces in human ills; and may be said to have been upon the staff of the hospitalizations that were established during that building up in that period.

The entity gained and lost, gained and lost, from its own soul development, while much of the material, of the world, those of carnal forces that go to make up carnal pleasures, came into the experience of the entity to *use*. Yet the *use* of same, *as* used, brought much of disturbing forces to the entity. While the abilities in the gathering of data, or experimental data in the application of much as may be termed as drugs in the present, were used in such work by the entity, and while to the world the entity meant much—to *self* the development was not beyond reproach.

The type of detail illustrated above, including past names, is not an uncommon finding in the life readings. These chronicles vividly depict the role of karma and the necessity of reincarnation to allow the soul to learn, rectify past errors, and improve in spirit and godliness. The estimated number of life readings approached 2,500. Although Edgar and his family were initially reluctant to accept the notion of reincarnation, the evidence eventually won them over. The rationality of this premise was validated by the *Bible*, as we shall soon see.

I mentioned previously that the major Western religions do not teach or endorse reincarnation or karma. This view came about when, in 553 A.D., the Second Council of Constantinople dictated that these philosophies were church anathema. Despite this mandate, numerous indirect references to reincarnation and karma have survived in the *Bible* and related writings, but even the astute reader must search to discern them. Once the true meaning of these passages is revealed, you will realize that reincarnation or karma is the topic under discussion. Let us now examine some of these cryptic passages:[72]

> If any harm follows, then you shall give life for life, eye for eye, tooth for tooth, hand for hand, foot for foot, burn for burn, wound for wound, stripe for stripe. [Example of karma from the Old Testament] Exodus 21:24-25

> Jesus answered him, "Truly, truly, I say to you, unless one is born anew [reference to the need for reincarnation], he

cannot see the kingdom of God." Nicodemus said to him, "How can a man be born when he is old?" . . . Jesus answered, ". . . Do not marvel that I said to you, 'You must be born anew.' The wind blows where it wills, and you hear the sound of it, but you do not know whence it comes or whither it goes; so it is with every one who is born of the Spirit." Nicodemus said to him, "How can this be?" Jesus answered him, ". . . If I have told you earthly things and you do not believe, how can you believe if I tell you heavenly things?" John 3:3-12

"Truly, truly, I [Jesus] say to you, before Abraham was, I am." [Excerpt indicating that Jesus had lived prior to Abraham] John 8:58

As he [Jesus] passed by, he saw a man blind from his birth. And his disciples asked him, "Rabbi, who sinned, this man or his parents, that he was born blind?" Jesus answered, "It was not that this man sinned, or his parents, but that the works of God might be made manifest in him." [Passage consistent with the concept of karma for the blind man] John 9:1-3

Jesus said to her, "Your brother [Lazarus] will rise again." Martha said to him, "I know that he will rise again in the resurrection at the last day." Jesus said to her, "I am the resurrection and the life; he who believes in me, though he die, yet shall he live, and whoever lives and believes in me shall never die." [Reference suggestive of reincarnation] John 11:23-26

"And in anger his lord delivered him to the jailers, till he should pay all his debt. So also my heavenly Father will do to every one of you, if you do not forgive your brother from your heart." [Example of karma] Matthew 18:34-35

"Make friends quickly with your accuser, while you are going with him to court, lest your accuser hand you over to the judge, and the judge to the guard, and you be put in prison; truly, I say to you, you will never get out till you have paid the last penny." [Karma] Matthew 5:25-26

"Behold, I will send you Elijah the prophet before the great and terrible day of the Lord comes." [Foretelling the reincarnation of Elijah (next excerpts)] Malachi (Old Testament) 4:5

[Angel speaking to Zechariah about his future son, John the Baptist] "And he will turn many of the sons of Israel to the Lord their God, and he will go before him in the spirit and power of Elijah." [reincarnation of Elijah] Luke 1:17

"Truly, I [Jesus] say to you, among those born of women there has risen no one greater than John the Baptist ... For all the prophets and the law prophesied until John; and if you are willing to accept it, he is Elijah who is come. He who has ears to hear, let him hear." [Reincarnation] Matthew 11:11-15

And after six days Jesus took with him Peter and James and John his brother, and led them up a high mountain apart. And he was transfigured before them, and his face shone like the sun, and his garments became white as light. [Note also the repeated comparison to light.] And behold, there appeared to them Moses and Elijah, talking with him ... And as they were coming down the mountain ... the disciples asked him, "Then why do the scribes say that first Elijah must come?" He replied, "Elijah does come, and he is to restore all things; but I tell you that Elijah has already come, and they did not know him, but did to him whatever they pleased. So also the Son of man will suffer at their hands." Then the disciples understood that he was speaking of John the Baptist. [Excerpt again referring to Elijah's reincarnation as John the Baptist] Matthew 17:1-13

And they asked him, "Why do the scribes say that first Elijah must come?" And he said to them, "Elijah does come first to restore all things; ... But I tell you that Elijah has come, and they did to him whatever they pleased, as it is written of him." Mark 9:11-13

A generation goes, and a generation comes, but the earth remains forever.
  The sun rises and the sun goes down, and hastens to the place where it rises ...
  What has been is what will be, and what has been done is what will be done; and there is nothing new under the sun. Is there a thing of which it is said, "See, this is new?" It has been already, in the ages before us.
  There is no remembrance of former things, nor will there

be any remembrance of later things yet to happen among those who come after. [Reference to reincarnation and the loss of memory of past lives] Ecclesiastes (Old Testament) 1:4-11

And they asked him [John the Baptist], "What then? Are you Elijah?" He said, "I am not." "Are you the prophet?" And he answered, "No." They said to him then, "Who are you? Let us have an answer for those who sent us. What do you say about yourself?" He said, "I am the voice of one crying in the wilderness, 'Make straight the way of the Lord,' as the prophet Isaiah said." [Selection displaying John the Baptist's inability to remember his past life as Elijah] John 1:21-27

"Immediately after the tribulation of those days the sun will be darkened, and the moon will not give its light, and the stars will fall from heaven, and the powers of the heavens will be shaken; then will appear the sign of the Son of man in heaven, and then all the tribes of the earth will mourn, and they will see the Son of man coming on the clouds of heaven with power and great glory ... Truly, I say to you, this generation will not pass away till all these things take place." [Last sentence referring to reincarnation continuing until the time of the tribulation] Matthew 24:29-34

Then Jesus said to him, "Put your sword back into its place; for all who take the sword will perish by the sword." [Karma] Matthew 26:52

Peter began to say to him, "Lo, we have left everything and followed you." Jesus said, "Truly, I say to you, there is no one who has left house or brothers or sisters or mother or father or children or lands, for my sake and for the gospel, who will not receive a hundredfold now in this time, houses and brothers and sisters and mothers and children and lands, with persecutions, and in the age to come eternal life. But many that are first will be last, and the last first." [Reference to karma and reincarnation] Mark 10:28-30

[She] brought forth a male child, one who is to rule all the nations with a rod of iron, but her child was caught up to God and to his throne . . . [passage asserting the acceptance of reincarnation during the time this book was written] Revelation 12:5

If any one is to be taken captive, to captivity he goes; if anyone slays with sword, with the sword must he be slain. [Karma] Revelation 13:10

Do not be deceived; God is not mocked, for whatever a man sows, that he will also reap. [Karma] Galatians 6:7

"Watch and pray that you may not be born in the flesh, but that you may leave the bitter bondage of this life" [passage implying that the cycle of reincarnation ends when the state of godliness is achieved] Book of Thomas the Contender (Gnostic Gospel) 9:5[73]

Jesus says: "There is nothing buried which shall not be raised up." [reincarnation] Greek papyrus Oxyrhynchus 654[74]

Thus it is written, "The first man Adam became a living being; the last Adam became a life-giving spirit." [Reincarnation; reference to Christ?] 1 Corinthians 15:45

The last passage from Corinthians suggests that Christ may have been a reincarnation of Adam. Note that the Source, in the following Cayce reading, also supports this doctrine:

(Q) Please give the important re-incarnations of Adam in the world's history.
(A) [Cayce] In the beginning as Amilius, as Adam, as Melchizedek, as Zend [?], as Ur [?] [Enoch? GD's[75] note: Perhaps Ur was prehistory person [364-9, Par. 3-A] who established Ur of the Chaldees? I don't think he was mentioned anywhere else in the readings as an incarnation of Jesus.], as Asaph [?] [Songs of Asaph? See Ps. 81:5 indicating that Joseph and Asaph were one and the same?], as Jesus [Jeshua]—Joseph—Jesus. [See 364-9, Par. 3-A.]
    Then, as that coming into the world in the second coming—for He will come again and receive His own, who have prepared themselves through that belief in Him and acting in that manner; for the *spirit* is abroad, and the time draws near, and there will be the reckoning of those

even as in the first so in the last, and the last shall be first; for there is that Spirit abroad—He standeth near. He that hath eyes to see, let him see. He that hath ears to hear, let him hear that music of the coming of the Lord of this vineyard, and art *Thou* ready to give account of that *thou* hast done with thine opportunity in the earth as the Sons of God, as the heirs and joint heirs of glory *with* the Son? Then make thine paths straight, for there must come an answering for that *Thou* hast done with thine Lord! He will not tarry, for having overcome He shall appear even *as* the Lord *and* Master. Not as one born, but as one that returneth to His own, for He will walk and talk with men of every clime, and those that are faithful and just in their reckoning shall be caught up with Him to rule and to do *judgment* for a thousand years!   364-7

Thus, it becomes clear that both the *Bible* and the Cayce readings discuss and support the concepts of reincarnation and karma. Certainly, we can see how these topics were so stealthily broached in the pages of the *Bible*.

In the following two Cayce readings, the Source introduces the concept that the soul–spirit (pre–birth) freely and voluntarily makes the choice as to the body it will inhabit, its choice of parents, environment, handicaps, etc., for its next life:

In giving the interpretations of the records as we find here of the sojourns in the earth, the activities of the entity in the environs about the earth, these are rather inclinations. And the will of self in its activity as regards that the entity sets as its ideal [that is, its choices] makes for the developments or retardments in the present experience. What the entity has been [past incarnations] makes an influence about the same as what an entity studies[,] inclines or induces the trend of thought, or the thinking becomes along given lines, controlled by will and the ideal as chosen by the entity.   1261-1

For, there is ever the choice by the soul-entity as to the environs, as to the path to be taken in its application of opportunities *expressed* in material consciousness.   2650-1

The above passages offer the necessary theological background for the Source's repeated discussions on karma. The Source frequently noted that karma was the reason for many afflictions affecting those receiving life or physical readings. Examples are numerous. In the next selections, I list the patient's condition first (in brackets), followed by the Source's explanation:

[Multiple sclerosis] Before this, then, the entity was in the land of the present sojourn, in those associations with the activities in the struggle for freedom on the part of some with whom the entity joined; yet the mercilessness of the savage (as would be termed in the present) was indicated in the orders given by the entity in dealing with characters and activities. And these rendered many helpless. Ye are meeting same in thine own self [the Source's words for describing karma]. And some of those upon whom ye meted those measures must today measure to thee in patience.   2564-3

[Epilepsy] The sources of these disturbances should be as much of a problem, not so much as to cause too great a concern but to know that these are for those responsible for the body as well as for the body itself. Hence these are karmic. It is faith alone that can bring all of these things to pass in these experiences of this body, without there being after effects. It is true that healing of body, of mind, of the effects, can be accomplished in faith alone. Yet, as in every individual experience that is a manifestation in the earth, there is the physical and the mental to be dealt with. These need manifestations even as He manifested in flesh—though divine; that we as individuals through Him might know the way back to God.   3210-2

[Baby with Down's syndrome] Here we find an individual entity born not only to be a charge to the parents but it [karma] is needed for the parents, as well as needed by the entity.   5335-1

[Metastatic melanoma (cancer)] EC: (In undertone—"What a poor station!") Yes, we have the body here ... As we find, there are disturbing conditions. This disturbance is of a nature that by some would be called karmic. Hence it is something the body *physically,* mentally, must meet, in its spiritual attitude first; that is: as the body may dedicate its

life and its abilities to a definite service, to the Creative
Forces or God, there will be healing forces brought to the
body.   3121-1

[Brain lesion] As we find, here we have a lesion in the
brain centers. This causes not only these spells of lapse of
control of the body but the inability for the body to control
itself in an emotional manner. This is a karmic condition.
                                                         3158-1

[Child with polio, paralyzed from the waist down]
(Q) Where did the child contract this disease that caused
the condition?
(A) The influence was abroad; and the body is meeting
those experiences within itself through which each entity, each soul must pass for its *own* soul development.
                                                          735-1

[Unknown tumors] As we find, conditions here indicate
sarcoma—that is a part of the karma of this body. These
may be aided, but as to correcting entirely—the suggested
applications will only be helpful for the conditions.
                                                         3387-1

[Phobia of noises]
(Q) How can I overcome my horror of noise and thunder-
storms? (I was always afraid of noise, but the fear of
thunder has been only in the last 15 or 20 years. If I did not
have this, I could manage better.)
(A) These are a part of thy consciousness from experiences
[past incarnations] in the material plane. Surround thyself at such times with the consciousness of a walk and
talk with Him, and noise and fear will be no more.
                                                         3161-1

[Obsessive-compulsive traits]
    Before this [the present incarnation] the entity was in
the French land . . .
    The activities then, as Count Dubourse [Dubois?] made
great contributions to the activities as related to *cleanliness*
as in relationship to disease; though the entity made no
pretenses, yet—as he indicated to others—he knew better
than others, and in *that* instance *did!* as to the needs of
same, especially as associated with or in activities related
to disease that could be transmuted, or those commonly

called the "catching" diseases; that these come not only from microbes but may be carried by individuals as well as by things.

Thus, in the present experience, it will be found that the entity will be inclined to be *clean* about its person . . .

2892-2

You will note, along with the explanations of the karmic conditions, that Cayce often reminds us that enlightenment and repayment of the karmic debt is necessary before the spirit can find its "way back to God." By understanding the concept of karma, we can better comprehend, as well as learn to improve, much of the complexity of our earthly lives.

Moreover, the readings teach us that all individuals select their personal circumstances for the next life, depending upon the particular lessons that need to be learned. Each person needs to undergo this educational and growth process to pay his or her respective karmic liability and achieve spiritual excellence. This same view is endorsed in several well-documented near-death scenarios, including that of Betty Eadie:

"I had seen people progressing in the worlds I had visited, working toward becoming more like our Father . . . They looked upon life here as a school where they could learn many things and develop the attributes they lacked. I was told that we had all *desired* to come here . . ."[76]

Lastly, before departing this topic, I have found that the concept of reincarnation explains one other controversial subject—homosexuality. The Source's view of reincarnation was that families and close friends were often reincarnated together in repeated life spans. A husband and wife in one lifetime might be, say, a man and close male colleague, respectively, in another incarnation. Thus, reincarnation presents itself as one rationalization for why a person in one life may have strong affections for another individual, if even of the same sex. Although a man or woman may never have displayed homosexual characteristics in previous lives, a subsequent incarnation may again find the individual strongly attracted to his or her soul mate—but now of the same gender! Food for thought . . .

9

Edgar Cayce Miscellany

*T*he purpose of this chapter is to provide a venue for concepts that did not consistently apply to other sections of this book. These topics include Source discussions on astrology, free will, prophecies and other revelations, imaginary friends of childhood, and prayer.

The following discussion on astrology will also demonstrate the ambiguous and equivocal nature of some of the readings.

ASTROLOGY AND THE SPIRITUAL DIMENSIONS

One aspect of the Cayce readings that originally troubled me (since I had never been an advocate of astrology) was the description of the planets of the solar system as representing eight dimensions, as expressed by Arthur Lammers in 1923:

"[The solar system] has eight dimensions, corresponding to the planets . . . This [the earth] is the third dimension, and it is a sort of laboratory for the whole system, because only here is free will com-

pletely dominant. On the other planes, or dimensions,
some measure of control is kept over the soul to see that it
learns the proper lessons."[77]

I wish to bring out several points here. First, mention is made of the
existence of only eight planets. (Pluto was not discovered until 1930.)
This detail should not present a problem with even current scientific
opinions, as astronomers have long believed Pluto to be either a massive comet or an escaped planetary satellite captured in orbit by the
sun's gravity.[78] Second, the discussion of free will remains controversial.
Two beliefs dominate this picture:

1. If, as some believe, predestination exists among entities that are
omniscient over all time frames (past, present, and future—such as God),
then free will becomes a relative concept. In other words, free will exists
for us, as humans, but not for God and other spiritual entities that exist
outside of time and space.

2. In contrast, the Source made it clear that future events and prophecies were never cast in stone. According to the Source, predestination
is not a factor or consideration. Humankind's ability for free will always
presents the possibility for change and, hence, makes the future an unknown. We will examine this topic in more detail in the next section,
"The Cayce Revelations."

Arthur Lammers, to whom the above quote is attributed, was the
individual who catalyzed Cayce's interest in performing life readings, as
opposed to the health-related or physical readings that had been ex-
clusively performed previously. In my attempt to verify the authenticity
of the above reading, I have yet to identify a comparable reference or
quote in any of my searches of the more than 14,000 catalogued readings. Cayce himself noted that he "could not find all the things Lammers
had mentioned."[79] However, in defense of Lammers, one much later reading from October 1935 (1021-3) bears some similarities:

And as materiality in the earth becomes of a three-
dimensional experience, so in other environs they become rather the dimensions of those planets in their

relationships to the activity of the soul in its application of understanding gained BY the soul in its search for, and in its application of, its relations to the Creative Force or Energies. Hence we have, in this [particular individual's] experience, Jupiter, Mercury, Saturn, Uranus; all becoming a portion of beneficent influences in the experience *innately* and manifestedly, in so far as the [individual] entertains and applies those influences in its relationships to a causation experience in the earth.

This excerpt may simply imply that the planets have effects from their astrologic potentials (as Cayce frequently alluded to in the readings), but it is also consistent with the former Lammers' description. Edgar's son, Hugh Lynn, agreed with the Lammers point of view (for example, see his letter following reading 1261-1[80]). Indeed, when the Source describes a "Mercurian," "Jupiterian," or any other planetary "sojourn or activity," perhaps it is referring to the spirit's personal journey *on that planet*, rather than the astrologic *influence of the planet on the person* in this lifetime. If the former is the case, then the previously noted descriptions of patients' past-life regressions, depicting beings of Light traveling from one planet to another, might well be accurate. In this case, the planets may well represent other spheres or planes through which we must progress before achieving the ultimate state of God-like perfection and nirvana. In *Many Mansions: The Edgar Cayce Story*, Gina Cerminara explained that the names of the planets were, instead, used metaphorically to describe "experiences in other dimensions of consciousness" [81] as handed down by tradition. Although I tend to favor this last interpretation, any of these explanations are plausible and cannot be dismissed.

In a separate reading, the Source discusses the Akashic Records. In this passage, I was struck by the Source's modern insight into quantum physics. What you will note is a complete grasp of Einstein's special theory of relativity, whereby the three spatial dimensions and time are viewed as mere variables in our universe:

... Not light years as the akashic records, or as the esoteric records, or as counted by astrology or astronomy, in the speed or the reflection of a ray of light; for, as records are made, the akashic records are as these:

Activity of *any* nature, as of the voice, as of a light made, produced in the natural forces those of a motion—which pass on, or are upon, the record of that as time . . . *it* passes even faster than time itself. Hence *light* forces pass much faster, but the records are upon the esoteric, or etheric, or akashic forces, as they go along upon the wheels of time, the wings of time, or in *whatever* dimension we may signify as a matter of its momentum or movement. Hence as the forces that are attuned to those various incidents, periods, times, places, may be accorded to the record, the *contact* as of the needle upon the record, as to how clear a rendition or audition is received, or how clear or how perfect an attunement of the instrument used as the reproducer of same is attuned to those *keepers*—as may be termed—*of* those records. What would be indicated by the keepers? That as just given, that they are the records upon the wings or the wheel of time itself. Time, as that as of space—as inter-between. That inter-between, that which is, that of which, that from one object to another when in matter is of the same nature, or what that is[,] is what the other is, only changed in its vibration to produce that element, or that force, as is termed in man's terminology as *dimensions* of space, or *dimensions* that give it, whatever may be the solid, liquid, gas, or what *its form* or dimension!

364-6

In this narrative, the Source is succinctly observing the obscure nature of space and time, as validated by Einstein. From the quantum perspective, light exists as the universal constant. When measuring the speed of light, regardless of the observer's speed or direction, light's speed (as measured in a vacuum) is always constant at 186,000 miles/second. What does change, however, when the observer approaches fractional speeds of light, is the *observer*! The observer's spatial dimensions decrease and time slows—relative to an observer at rest. Indeed, time and space are trivial variables compared to the significance of light. Space and time are dimensions restricted merely to our current realm of materiality.

THE CAYCE REVELATIONS

The Source made multiple prophecies and revelations throughout the course of the readings. This information related to such diverse topics as hidden treasures (including oil), Atlantis, war, pole shifts, and other climactic earth events. Many of these divinations have yet to be substantiated or, at the very least, have yet to occur. Many have already been confirmed as erroneous. Anticipating criticisms, however, the Source warned of two reasons for possible inaccuracies in these predictions:

1) The capacity of the human race for *free will* always exists as an unknown. That is to say, through free will, we always have the capability to change prophecy and alter the future:

> [God] Having given free will, then—though having the foreknowledge, though being omnipotent and omnipresent—it is only when the soul that is a portion of God *chooses* that God knows the end thereof. 5749-14

This is not the only paranormal source to discuss the power of human free will. During Dannion Brinkley's near–death experience, a being of Light revealed to him a multitude of prophesized events. However, the spirit also informed Brinkley, "The flow of human events can be changed"—that is, the outcomes were not inescapable. As humans, we are "great, powerful, and mighty spiritual Beings."[82]

2) The Source would not give predictions (for example, for the recovery of buried treasure or stock market fluctuations) intended for personal financial gain and gratification. The beneficiary would encounter success only if the proceeds were intended for truly unselfish and altruistic purposes. Any exception to this rule would inevitably lead to failure:

> Hence in such an approach, they each should weigh well in the balance as to whether there are ulterior motives [to using information from the readings] or whether they are of the nature that is rather just wonderment, and with

little thought or idea of what such information might put upon them as individuals. And again as to whether such would be used for that of personal gain, or is it to be given to all who would in themselves seek? . . . But with those same warnings that he that uses same for his own personal aggrandizement *does* so to his *own* undoing.   3976-16

After the market crash of 1929, a loss of funding forced Cayce's Virginia Beach hospital to close its doors. The hospital represented a lifetime of hopes and dreams for Cayce. In addition, the economic collapse impoverished Cayce and his family. In response, Cayce reluctantly acquiesced to give readings aimed at acquiring wealth. Such rewards, he hoped, would allow him to reopen the hospital and otherwise further his philanthropic work. It was for a humanitarian cause. These endeavors included treasure hunting at White Hill, Virginia; Kelly's Ford, Virginia; Washington County, Arkansas; the Lost Dutchman mine in Arizona; and oil in Texas. Despite all the good intentions, however, these attempts met with failure. Cayce could only conclude that someone, within each of these groups, lacked the pure motives required.

Keeping the above thoughts in mind, let us examine some of Cayce's additional visions. In the section that follows, bracketed notes are the addition of stenographer Gladys Davis.

In the following excerpt, Cayce forecasts a dramatic pole shift, which did not occur in 1936 as prophesied. Did the Source possibly intend the date as 2036?

And those that seek in the latter portion of the year of our Lord . . . '36, He [He, Christ Spirit?] will appear . . . The earth will be broken up in the western portion of America. The greater portion of Japan must go into the sea. The upper portion of Europe will be changed as in the twinkling of an eye. Land will appear off the east coast of America. There will be the upheavals in the Arctic and in the Antarctic that will make for the eruption of volcanos in the Torrid areas, and there will be shifting then of the poles— so that where there has been those of a frigid or the semitropical will become the more tropical, and moss and fern will grow. And these will begin in those periods in '58 to '98, when these will be proclaimed as the periods when His light will be seen again in the clouds.   3976-15

In the next passage, the Source responds to a question relating to the earth's geography "at the time of Atlantis' highest civilization:"

> As to the highest point of civilization, this would . . . depend upon whether we are viewing from a spiritual standpoint or upon that as a purely material or commercial standpoint; for the variations, as we find, extend over a period of some two hundred thousand years (200,000)—that is, as light years—as known in the present—and that there were *many* changes in the surface of what is now called the earth. In the first, or greater portion, we find that *now* known as the southern portions of South America and the Arctic or North Arctic regions, while those in what is *now* as Siberia—or that as of Hudson Bay—was rather in that region of the tropics, or that position now occupied by near what would be as the same *line* would run, of the southern Pacific, or central Pacific regions—and about the same way. Then we find, with this change that came first in that portion, when the first of those peoples used that as prepared FOR the changes in the earth, we stood near the same position as the earth occupies in the present—as to Capricorn, or the equator, or the poles. Then, with that portion, *then* the South Pacific, or Lemuria [?], began its disappearance—even before Atlantis, for the changes were brought about in the latter portion of that period, or what would be termed ten thousand seven hundred (10,700) light years, or earth years, or present setting of those, as set by Amilius [?]—or Adam.   364-4

In the next and last selection (from a reading on December 18, 1943), Cayce discloses information dealing with the end of World War II. Again, Gladys Davis has inserted some excellent, explanatory commentary:

> (Q) Is the prophecy still possible of fulfillment, of May 1941, that war against Germany will end in the spring of '44?
> (A) This will end in the spring of '44. [3/57 GD's note: The 1950 World Almanac indicates that Hitler was wounded in an attempted assassination July 20, 1944. It is possible that this planned assassination was seen. If it had gone through, war would have ended immediately—long before the invasion.]
> (Q) When will the war with Japan end?

(A) It will be much later, but more sudden in its close.
[First atomic bomb was dropped on Japan August 6,
1945; the second atomic bomb was dropped August 9,
1945. Japan surrendered August 14, 1945.]   257-254

From this last citation in particular, we see how humankind's free
will can intervene to change, or at least forestall (e.g., Germany's surren-
der), the future.

IMAGINARY FRIENDS

Imaginary friends are common among children, especially those believed to be loners, introverts, or perhaps just lacking in social skills.
Oddly, however, it can be argued that if these children are truly antiso-
cial, why would they involve themselves with even make-believe
people? Wouldn't they prefer to be apart from all children? I have no
doubt that any professional responses would involve discourses outlining the children's needs for interaction with colleagues of similar likes
and values, avoidance of conflict, and circumvention of the stresses of
social interaction. One other possible explanation remains, however.
Many, including myself, leave open the feasibility that *some* children
may actually be associating with true spirits—existing in the same hidden dimensions that also harbor the other spirit dimensions. Once
again, as a child, Edgar Cayce exemplified one such special child.

Edgar referred to his playmates as the "little folk." One of Edgar's
closest friends, Anna Seay, reportedly could also see and interact with
these companions. These two close friends spent countless hours with
these imaginary friends. Other friends and family could not see their
fanciful comrades, however, and Edgar soon learned not to discuss them,
except around Anna. The "little folk," however, did cease visiting Edgar
at age fourteen (1892), signifying the year that Anna died from pneu-
monia. Anna may well have been closer to the imaginary friends than
Edgar. What the significance of their abandonment at this time represents can only be conjectured. Certainly, the intimate association that
these illusory companions had upon Edgar and Anna for most of their
childhood must have been profound. We can all empathize with the
impact of close friendships on our own lives. As children, personal

bonds are often stronger and more intimate than the relationships we establish as adults. No doubt, our all-too-hectic adult work schedules do not encourage the formation of close individual friendships.

Cayce's metaphysical childhood experiences did not end here. He frequently saw and spoke with his deceased grandfather. The young Edgar had witnessed his violent death (a horsing accident) at the age of four.

In a separate incident, Edgar and Anna discovered a special life form that only they could see. Edgar characterized these creatures as "smaller than the little folks, but larger than insects."[83] These entities preferred to associate with plants, however—not humans.

PRAYER

Edgar Cayce and the Source were great advocates of prayer. Not only did Cayce promote prayer but in many readings he gave examples of model prayers:

Let this be the prayer with the entity, daily:
"Father, God! In Thy love, in Thy mercy, Thou hast given us the opportunity to see the manifestations of Thy love among men. Let us appreciate that opportunity Thou hast given. And may each of us, day by day, keep the faith in Him who has promised, 'Lo, I am with Thee always, even unto the end of the world.'" 2547-1

Let this, then, be thy prayer:
"Thou, O Lord, art holy in thine dealings with thy fellow man. I, O God, am Thine—body, mind and soul! *purge* thou me, that I may be one with Thee—and through that power Thou givest me make known to others the beauty, the love, thou hast shed on me." 264-45

Cayce taught not only that prayer was effective but that it was more efficacious when performed in quantity. This phenomenon represents one additional example of the truism "if one is good, more is definitely better."

And as of old, the prayers of ten may save a city; the

> prayers of twenty-five may save a nation . . . but in union
> there is strength.   1598-2

During my research, I was surprised to find a recurring relationship between prayer and the near–death experience. When I first read how one near–death victim observed prayers radiating from the earth as beams of light, I made a special mental note. The scenario impressed me, but I had not recalled any similar descriptions of prayers in reviews of other near–death experiences. I seldom give much credence to isolated events. However, time and additional scrutiny into the near–death phenomena have convinced me that our earthly prayers do indeed have substance and meaning, just as the Cayce readings suggest. I list below two identical, well–respected near–death visions by Betty Eadie and Dannion Brinkley:

> "I saw many lights shooting up from the earth like beacons . . . I was told that these beams of power were the prayers of people on earth." (Betty Eadie)[84]

> "[Prayers] were streaming through the heavenly world like rays of light. It was beautiful to see what becomes of our prayers." (Dannion Brinkley)[85]

I believe it unlikely that these visions were purely coincidental. Indeed, I am convinced that prayers are powerful and consequential and that they gain added influence in number.

10

Windows to God

*I*consider myself a somewhat intelligent individual. Yet despite considerable study and practice, I have failed miserably at being able to develop any amount of personal psychic potential. My experience has convinced me that psychic gifts are just that—gifts. I am well aware that the Source and other reputable psychics testify that such talents can be learned. Perhaps—and hopefully—in future years, I will agree. Many advocate that the ability to realize your full psychic potential is dependent purely upon your willingness to work and develop such a specific talent. Mastering any psychic ability is similar to the mastery of any school subject—for example, calculus. We all theoretically have the capability to learn and master calculus, but many of us find it nearly impossible to hone this skill to the point of excellence. For now, I must remain pacified by the fact that I—and anyone—can readily experience at least one aspect of the paranormal through a faculty that God has bestowed on us all—that is, dreams.

Dreams represent the common vehicle by which the ordinary individual can access the unconscious, and it is very simple. To start, however, we must first *remember* our dreams. Let's examine this elementary skill. In early 2003, I noted that I had not recalled a dream, seemingly, for months. My A.R.E. colleagues reminded me that I needed to take more of an active part in remembering my dreams. Specifically, dream experts recommend that you merely make a mental suggestion at bedtime to recall your dreams. Prior to writing this book, I had never attempted this effortless technique, and I had actually attributed my failure at remembering my dreams to my chaotic work schedule. I readily tried the suggestion, however, and was astounded at the result. I recalled that very night my first dream in months. Most dream experts recommend various techniques for remembering and analyzing dreams. These methods include the pre–sleep suggestion, keeping a dream journal, making entries during the night while the dream is still fresh, as well as a thoughtful analysis and interpretation of each dream.

The first step toward proper understanding of dreams is the recognition that most dreams are metaphorical in nature and should not be interpreted literally. There are innumerable dream interpretation books available, including those at the A.R.E. Bookstore and on the Internet. These books and information sources offer an excellent means to understanding your dreams. An indispensable constituent of your dream interpretation material includes a *dream dictionary*. A dream dictionary offers you the common metaphors recognized in dreams. One example is the car. It may represent a life's journey, your physical vehicle in life (i.e., your body), or even a personal character trait, such as integrity. Hence, dream interpretation is quite dependent upon the individual's own life's blessings, ordeals, and misfortunes at the time. Yet, the dream exists as an easily accessible window to the subconscious. This window may be opened to anyone willing to perform the elementary recommendations discussed above.

Dream experts suggest that dreams open a window into the subconscious, a realm that allows us to access the higher planes of existence. As such, we may sometimes connect directly, or indirectly (more commonly), to the thoughts of others, as well as information sources such as the collective unconscious. Dream authorities state that the nebulous and metaphorical visions we often encounter are the result of the more prevalent *indirect* communications we establish in dreams. Similar to

stories that we hear third–hand, these indirect communications may
not represent reality. Hence, dream interpretation must be made
thoughtfully and seldom literally. We tend to experience the more rare,
direct visions during times of intense stress, such as during the illness of
a loved one. Death–related visions are classic examples of this type of
phenomenon, and, occasionally, we do not even require the sleep state
to establish these intimate links. These visions may be quite detailed
and accurate, not dissimilar from the out–of–body experiences of near–
death victims.

Cayce also had an opinion on the significance of the dream state. The
Source specifically noted that the soul departs its earthly body during
dreams:

(Q) Do I actually leave my body at times, as has been
indicated, and go to different places?
(A) [Cayce] You do.
(Q) For what purpose, and how can I develop and use this
power constructively?
(A) Just as has been given as to how to enter into
meditation. Each and every soul leaves the body as it rests
in sleep.
    As to how this may be used constructively—this would
be like answering how could one use one's voice for
constructive purposes. It is of a same or of a similar import,
you see; that is, it is a faculty, it is an experience, it is a
development of the self as related to spiritual things,
material things, mental things.
    Then as to the application of self in those directions for
a development of same—it depends upon what is the
purpose, what is the desire. Is it purely material? Is it in
that attitude, "If or when I am in such and such a position
I can perform this or that"? If so, then such expressions are
only excuses within self—in any phase of an experience.
    For as He has given, it is here a little, there a little—Use
that you have in hand today, NOW, and when your
abilities and activities are such that you may be entrusted
with other faculties, other developments, other experiences, they are a part of self.
    As to how it may be used: Study to show thyself
approved unto God, a workman not ashamed of that you
think, of that you do, or of your acts; keeping self unspot-
ted from your own consciousness of your ideal; having the

> courage to dare to do that you know is in keeping with
> God's will.   853-8

From a personal standpoint, I appreciate dreams as my only consistent, *recognized*, psychic gift. For this, I am grateful. The dream–state may well represent the sole mechanism (for many) by which to navigate the uncharted waters of our ultimate reality. I will now relate one of my own experiences. Prior to writing *God at the Speed of Light*, I had one recurrent dream. In it, I was again a college student back at Vanderbilt. In this dream, I found I was consistently missing important classes, including tests. I was constantly combating the fear of being kicked out of school and not fulfilling my lifelong ambition of becoming a doctor. When I would awake from these episodes, I would typically feel mentally exhausted and physically fatigued. This is a common dream experience. The most common interpretation is that the dreamer is anxious about completing a present–day task, similar to the test anxiety experienced during previous school years. I interpreted these dreams to mean that I had yet an unfinished purpose in my life. The dream symbolically represented my current failure (and anxiety) over having not yet achieved that goal.

Then, in December 2003, as I was completing the text that you now read, I had the following dream: I was in my medical residency. (Apparently, I had finally finished college!) In this new phase of my education, I found I was repeatedly missing important meetings. Now my residency was at risk. However, I found some comfort in knowing that the particularly critical learning phases of my life had been successfully completed. Even if I failed my medical residency, I still had innumerable medical options remaining. I could reapply for a medical residency, enter a new medical specialty, or even enter any number of other medically related fields. I interpreted this new vision as indicating that I was headed in the proper developmental direction—spiritually. I had progressed in my life's purpose but had not yet completed it. I believed that the dream was offering me a degree of comfort, while at the same time prompting me to continue my present course. Of course, I am aware that my explanation is certainly subject to other equally sound interpretations. However, I believe this series of events represents one further example of God's willingness to communicate with us if we are receptive to hearing Him.

In conclusion, let us not discount the importance of dreams. Although we may not wish to interpret a dream literally, it may still contain an important message.

CAN THIS TECHNIQUE BE LEARNED?

Edgar Cayce displayed several psychic gifts: (1) He could view spirits in hidden dimensions (e.g., the "little folk" and his deceased grandfather). (2) He could learn the contents of a book by just sleeping on it. (3) He was a clairvoyant when in trance. I find it hard to imagine that the average individual could learn all of these talents. Yet some people believe that all of us have the psychic potential to do just that!

My own experiences indicate that these talents are either gifted by God or are gained through extraordinary, usually traumatic, life-shattering events. Hearing the tale of a psychic or supernatural ability being gained as the result of an NDE is not uncommon. Likewise, there are cases where the attribute is acquired through physical trauma or affliction (e.g., epilepsy), without mention of an associated NDE. Perhaps the victim denies the NDE (due to credibility fears) or otherwise erases it from memory. Maybe the NDE is not a prerequisite at all.

Kimberly Clark Sharp developed the ability to visualize spirits following her near-death experience. Simultaneously, a doctor also diagnosed her with a medical condition known as narcolepsy. This condition is associated with hypnagogic (i.e., just prior to sleep) hallucinations, to which she initially ascribed her visions. Thus, skeptics can attribute her visions to the medical illness. Proponents can credit her gift to the NDE. Despite treatment for her condition, however, Sharp continued visualizing this spiritual dimension.[86]

Best-selling author and medium James Van Pragh believes that all persons have some degree of psychic ability:

> "I am often asked if I was born a medium or if I was transformed into one by a terrible illness, or a freak accident that caused some sort of head trauma, or a near-death experience. As hair-raising as those possibilities may be, I cannot claim any one of them as the dramatic

moment that introduced me to my life's work . . .
        "We are all born with some level of psychic ability. The
question is: Do we recognize our psychic abilities and act
upon them?"[87]

In their books, both Sharp and Van Pragh come across as caring and
genuine. Regarding all accounts of such psychic phenomena, just as
with reports of radical, new scientific discoveries, I encourage the reader
to stay ever vigilant and yet to keep an open mind—as both cynic and
advocate. For those interested, the Committee for the Scientific Investigation of Claims of the Paranormal (CSICOP) maintains an active
website (www.csicop.org) on the Internet. This site gives a convincing
skeptic's analysis of such claims (though at times extreme). As always,
any unproven critique should undergo the same intense scrutiny as
any new theory.

From the medical and scientific standpoints, there are several theories for why trauma or disease might unveil a psychic or paranormal
window into a concealed dimension. An incomplete listing includes the
following:

1) Nonspecific physical trauma of any type may induce a state of
medical shock (or low blood pressure). Specifically, any cause of reduced blood flow to the brain (including stroke) exposes this precious
organ to injury.

2) Comparable to hypotension, any cause of generalized oxygen
deprivation (e.g., pulmonary or heart disease) may produce similar central nerve damage.

3) Any type of direct physical injury may produce subtle or, at the
other end of the spectrum, extensive brain injury. Some causes of direct
brain injury encompass trauma, invasive cancers, infiltrative diseases,
and infection.

Many of these conditions overlap in their form of injury. For instance, a cancer may also impede blood flow to the brain. The injury
may not even be apparent from the objective viewpoint or by any observer. However, the death, injury, or chemical alteration of even a small
number of central nerve cells may modify sensitive thought pathways,

SEEKING INFORMATION ON

holistic health, spirituality, dreams, intuition or ancient civilizations?
Call 1-800-723-1112, visit our Web site, or mail in this postage-paid card for a FREE catalog of books and membership information.

Name: _____

Address: _____

City: _____

State/Province: _____

Postal/Zip Code: _____ Country: _____

Association for Research and Enlightenment, Inc.
215 67th Street
Virginia Beach, VA 23451-2061

For faster service, call 1-800-723-1112.
www.edgarcayce.org

PBIN

BUSINESS REPLY MAIL

FIRST CLASS   PERMIT NO. 2456   VIRGINIA BEACH, VA

POSTAGE WILL BE PAID BY ADDRESSEE

**ASSOCIATION FOR RESEARCH
AND ENLIGHTENMENT INC
215 67TH STREET
VIRGINIA BEACH VA 23451-9819**

mechanisms, and/or physiologic processes. Such hypothetical changes could then initiate the crucial cycle, immediate or otherwise, leading to the rending of the psychic or spiritual curtain.

Edgar Cayce, at age three, suffered a traumatic, serious head injury. A nail pierced his skull, possibly initiating his astonishing, metaphysical journey.

11

Death, Heaven, and Hell

*H*opefully, by now, you will have at least *considered* the possibility of reincarnation to explain the excerpts listed in Chapter 8. The more I read, the more I am convinced that reincarnation is the missing link that (1) supports the cited passages from the *Bible*, (2) explains the apparent injustices of life (as well as such narratives from the *Bible* as the "Book of Job"), (3) endorses Cayce's life readings, and (4) explains the past-life regressions of hypnotherapy.

The fact that there exists a close association between light and various paranormal experiences (including most near-death experiences, Cayce's clairvoyance channel, and some incarnations) should come as no surprise. Light plays a very special role in the spirit and supernatural realms.

For those who may still remain skeptical, I pose the following hypothetical scenario for you to consider. Imagine, for the time being, that there is no God. The scientific community has available evidence that all matter (via $E = mc^2$) will, over billions and billions of years, eventually degrade to electromagnetic radiation or pure energy ("E" or light). Hence, even atheists should accept that our physical bodies will, after death and an immense period

of time, decompose into pure light. When we reach this state, our transfigured bodies (not to mention our souls) will find it possible to transverse the entire universe at light speed. At this point, time becomes
nonexistent. When an entity travels without time restrictions, it has the
ability—or, more correctly, the requirement—to be everywhere at once.
This is omnipresence. Note that omnipresence, which exists coincident
with the past, present, and future, equates to omniscience. The only
entity with these attributes, according to our concept, is God. Thus, I
theorize that all matter—organic and mineral, living and nonliving—
will ultimately transcend to a likeness *approaching* that of God. I say
"approaching" only because there is so much information that we lack.
This hypothesis does not imply that we can live our lives without principles and morals and do whatever we please. I believe, although I cannot prove, that God exercises His power for supreme justice over those
who are not repentant or righteous. Certainly, reincarnation and karma
fit into this overall plan of learning and achievement. If the above scenario is literally factual, perhaps the righteous achieve nirvana billions
of years before the wicked. Or perhaps there is a Hell—another controversial subject. Just as there are different races and colors of people,
there are different wavelengths and frequencies of light. Just because all
matter will degrade to light doesn't imply that Hitler's spirit (following
his final incarnation?) will be of the same denomination of photon as
Mother Theresa's. In further support of this philosophy, several Eastern
religions promote the existence of varying spiritual hierarchies or planes
of being.

As we shall see, some corrupt and incorrigible spirits may deliberately choose Hell over Heaven, consciously wishing to side with Satan
and his angels.

The Source defined Hell as the spirit's separation from the "at–oneness with that divine Creative Energy, or from God" (900–282). In another reading, Cayce clarifies that this division from God is voluntary:

(Q) Is it the destiny of every spiritual entity to eventually
become one with God?
(A) [Cayce] Unless that entity wills its banishment. As is
given with man, in the giving of the soul, the will,
wherewith to manifest in the entity, whether spiritual,

whether material. With that, the entity, either spiritual or physical, may banish itself. Again a compliance with law; as has been given, Hell [was] prepared for Satan and his angels, yet God has not *willed* that *any* soul should perish. Giving of will to His creation, Man, that man might be one with Him, giving man the privilege of exercising his (man's) will, or exercising His (God's) will to be one with Him. 900-20

From the above selection, one would expect that Heaven represents the ultimate union with God. The Source, however, makes a distinction between the kingdom of Heaven and the kingdom of God:

In making self selfless[,] selfishness is obliterated, that there may be the activity of the ideal, and being led then by the spirit of truth gains the understanding of the ideal in its operation upon the lives and activities of individuals; . . . through faith leads on to the opening of the ways in virtue, understanding and patience, in which all become the more conscious of that oneness with the Father, so that as we are known of the Father so may we know the Father, thus making in the material activities of the mental and the conscious mind those channels that we as individuals . . . become channels that the way may be known to others; thus entering into the kingdom of heaven.
This variation differentiates the kingdom of heaven from the kingdom of the Father: One is the experiences of the finite. The other is the glory with the Oneness in the infinite.
Thus, as individuals become aware of these activities, the kingdom of heaven is within. 262-29

In a later reading, the Source elucidates that a person must experience the kingdom of Heaven before entering the kingdom of God. In other words, to gain entry into "the Kingdom of God—they that enter in have known the Happiness of the Kingdom of Heaven in their *own* experience" (262-111). The next excerpt reaffirms that the location of Heaven is within the human soul:

As the presence of the Father, as the presence of the Christ-Consciousness is everywhere present, . . . [the passage,] "I

have not yet ascended to my Father" would to some
indicate that the heaven and the Father are somewhere
else—a place of abode, the center about which all universal forces, all energies must turn or give off from. Hence
"up" may be rather from within, or to the within—of
which each soul is to become aware. For heaven is that
place, that awareness where the Soul—with all its attributes, its Mind, its Body—becomes aware of being in
the presence of the Creative Forces, or one with same. That
is heaven.   262-88

Thus, the Akashic Records indicate that Heaven is an experience that
we acquire prior to death, not after death. From this perspective, I equate
Heaven to the earthly state of enlightenment or spiritual rebirth. In
contrast, we become eligible to enter the kingdom of God only after
paying off all karmic debt and achieving piety.

Before ending our contemplation of death, let us review a dream that
Edgar Cayce reported during one physical reading. In this dream, Cayce
meets Death and is struck by Death's vitality:

You are not as ordinarily pictured—with a black mask or
hood, or as a skeleton, or like Father Time with a sickle.
Instead, you are fair, rose-cheeked, robust . . .
  [Death responds,] Yes, Death is not what many seem to
think. It is not the horrible thing which is often pictured.
                                                209-1

SEPTEMBER 11

September 11 signifies a horrific date for the 21st century. This was
the date when good confronted the worst in humankind. More people
died on this date than at Pearl Harbor, yet the evil we countered appeared far more sinister than that of the past Japanese Empire. The evil
paralleled more that of the German Third Reich and the atrocities committed at the German concentration camps. How is it possible that such
hatred could exist in the world? Certainly, if reincarnation and karma
truly endure, something seems to have gone horribly amiss. Had the
terrorists learned nothing in their previous incarnations? For believers
in reincarnation, lingering questions persist. Were some of those who

perished on 9-11 fulfilling past karmic debts? Or, perhaps, were many on that fateful day completing a more peaceful[88] and expeditious exit from this earthly realm than they would have otherwise—and were, paradoxically, blessed? Moreover, did those who committed these heinous acts procure monumental, future karmic liabilities? My convictions lead me to believe that the answer to many of these questions may be yes. Some, who might have otherwise suffered slow, painful deaths, say, to cancer, died suddenly and painlessly. It is even possible that their prebirth spirits had agreed to this climactic scenario. One point to this chapter is that even the vilest of crimes has a reason. We fall far short of being capable of understanding the justification for such acts—only God knows. Yet why would God try our patience and sanity in this manner? Again, we cannot and should not judge God, anymore than we cannot and should not judge others. We are much too naive and ignorant, on a spiritual basis, to approach this level of understanding. This type of fidelity may require a leap of faith, but these issues remain consistent with the postulates outlined in the Cayce life readings.

From a personal perspective, I believe that evil in the world emanates from the weakness and defilement of humankind and, possibly, the devil, if he indeed exists. Earthquakes and natural calamities, however, represent another subject of controversy, which may or may not involve the hand of God. Hence, whether in action or reaction, God may intervene in select circumstances (perhaps through prayer)—albeit in mysterious and often incomprehensible ways. For September 11, we can only guess at the possibilities.

I would now like to relate a personal story dealing with September 11. In May of 2001, our only child graduated from the University of Vermont. Following graduation, he was accepted for a prestigious finance position in Manhattan. His offices were located a short distance from the World Trade Center. During the summer of 2001, I visited him at his workplace. The financial district, its history, and its diversity mesmerized me. During the visit, I marveled at the architectural beauty, immensity, and splendor of the World Trade Center towers, and we ate a memorable lunch at its renowned restaurant, Windows on the World. Only during such a visit could one appreciate the enormity and grandeur of these great structures—110 stories each—each floor manifesting an acre in size.

During a visit home the first week of September 2001, our son surprised us with a ghostly, recurring dream he had been having for the preceding several months, and he didn't know what to make of it. This was his dream:

> He was aboard an airplane. As he peered out the window, he viewed what appeared to be swampland below. As the flight continued, he sensed that something was terribly wrong with the plane—it was going down. The jet was going to crash! Then . . . everything went black. He "awoke"—but still within the confines of the dream. His spirit now hovered outside of his body. In this new dimension, he felt the typical warmth, peace, and love of the near-death encounter—but there was no tunnel—no light. As he acquired a more lucid orientation, he was astounded to find that he was embodied within a painting—a portrait of himself—hanging on a wall. As he attempted to decipher what was transpiring, my wife and I unexpectedly appeared to greet him. We embraced, as spirits. We were together in Heaven, and all was love. At this point, the dream ended.

Although at first I found the dream surprising and confusing, I subsequently surveyed it from a more comforting perspective. In the past, I had always had some personal trepidation about the publication of *God at the Speed of Light*. What if I was wrong regarding the intimate relationship between God and Light? Would God be offended? Was the book supporting the concept of God under erroneous pretenses, which might be abhorrent to God? From this dream, I found peace in the literal depiction of our family in Heaven. I took comfort that my conclusions had been accurate. However, the vision gained added meaning after 9-11.

On the morning of September 11, our son exited the subway from the underground structure of the World Trade Center. That particular morning, he happened to have a meeting just down the street from the WTC, at the Downtown Athletic Club. As he crossed in the shadows of the Twin Towers, the first plane struck the South Tower. The debris from the explosion shattered windows on the streets below, all about him. The rest is unpalatable history. Our son was one of the fortunate, but like many of his colleagues, he personally saw and experienced the extraordinary terror of that day.

After September 11, 2001, his recurrent dream ceased. Viewing the event retrospectively, I renewed the earlier questions of its meaning. Perhaps, like many dreams involving vehicular crashes or death, it merely indicated an important transition from one life phase to another. Whatever its true meaning, it remains one of the most remarkable dreams in our family's history.

I cannot leave the subject of 9–11 without addressing the significance of what I refer to as the "9–11 serendipities." The 9–11 serendipities occurred precisely one year after September 11, 2001. The first took place on the close of market trading, September 10, 2002. On this date, the September Standard and Poor's 500 futures contract closed at exactly 911.00. Note that it did not close at 910.99 or even 911.01. Questions of collusion and price-fixing arose, but none was ever reported. I continue to question whether such a combination of factors, premeditated or otherwise, could have, even intentionally, produced such an exceptional result.

The second 9–11 serendipity is just as uncanny. On September 11, 2002, the New York State Lottery produced the following winning number combination: 911. Again, the number was not 119 or 191, but 911—and in New York! The 14,878 winners, all who had selected 911 as their lucky lottery number on that anniversary date, shared the $4,999,990 lottery amount. Did these events represent selective interventions on God's part? If so, why? I surmise that God may have just been reminding humankind that He had not forgotten or abandoned us. For those who believe that the events were just the result of pure chance, they were certainly nothing short of miraculous.

12

Conclusions

As we have already determined, Edgar Cayce, with his phe-nomenal clairvoyance, was decades ahead of his time. His hu-mility, generosity, selflessness, and initial disbelief of the credibil-ity of his own readings made him a likable and identifiable figure. His humanity was revealed by his own failure to follow the Source's recommendations (for example, diet). From a humanitar-ian standpoint, however, Edgar Cayce aimed to successfully emu-late the Man he most worshiped—that is, Christ. Edgar Cayce came as close as any human to achieving this goal.

I have strived to present both sides of the Cayce coin, but there is no mistaking that his intent was always to benefit humankind through his service. Despite the rare refund requests and dissatis-fied recipients of the readings, most were quite satisfied and ap-preciative. The case of epileptic Aimee Dietrich (previously discussed, 2473-1) is an extraordinary testimonial to the success of the readings. The benevolence and benefit spread by Edgar Cayce over his lifetime is well documented in books that I recommend, particularly Sugrue's *The Story of Edgar Cayce: There Is a River* and Kirkpatrick's *Edgar Cayce: An American Prophet*. I did not attempt to

135

duplicate their stories here. However, I wish to end this text by listing comments and testimonials, such as the following, which are common-place addenda to many of the readings:

> "She had the osteopathic adjustments as directed and was almost immediately relieved of the spasms of coughing. She recovered completely." (4943-1)

> "One of the physicians who made the examination told me that Mr. Cayce's diagnosis was very accurate; that his psychic powers in this connection were in evidence and beyond question . . . There is no question in my mind as to Mr. Cayce's psychic powers, and as to his honesty and sincerity there is not a shadow of a doubt. I have abundant evidence to confirm this belief." [He has the above letter witnessed by a Notary Public.[89]] (4955-1)

> "Dr. [4135] is still living and is enthusiastic about EC's work. He sent many people to EC through the years to obtain readings." (4135-1)

> "I think I can safely predict complete success for the recovery of the baby in every phase of this injury and its sundry complications . . . People like me wish Godspeed to people like you—warmest personal regards and greetings to Tom Sugrue—likewise best wishes for your family from one of your most sincere believers." (2178-1)

> "I do not know of any words or enough money to express my appreciation and thanks." (779-22)

> "I have great faith in your powers and I am sure now that you will soon be able to record this case as a cure. After the above history, nobody could deny that your efforts were directly responsible for any cure. May God be good to you and keep you with us for many years to come. We all need you. Sincerely, [4020]." (4020-1)

> "First of all, I wish to thank you for your diagnosis and treatment and tell you how much it has done for me. I have been greatly helped and benefitted [sic] by the treatment so far, and with your assurance that cases like mine have been cured, am sure that I also can be *entirely* relieved." (283-1)

"The Reading was certainly wonderful and told just what was the trouble . . . May God bless you with health and strength, to carry on your wonderful work." (3160-1)

"[When] I begin to pick out the 12 greatest men—men who have [benefited] humanity—I know one who will head the list, and that person will be your Most Royal Highness—in other words Mr. Cayce himself . . . I can certainly see a great deal of improvement in my health, many thanks to you, Mr. Cayce (most of my time and money has been spent, visiting [doctors'] offices and then more [doctors'] offices)." (1713-1)

Even after his death, Edgar Cayce continues to have a profound effect on those seeking his aid. The following testimonial represents just one of many instances of the continuing benefit of his God–given gift:

July 19, 1968, Letter from Mrs. Ann Milano to Dr. H. J. Reilly: "Another Cayce remedy, 5057-1, has also helped my husband. It was wonderful of you to obtain it for him. Since my husband came to see you last August, he has been improving all the time—hasn't taken any drugs whatsoever. It is a miracle! After all, he has only been sick for twenty years! The doctors discovering only four years ago that it was colitis! It was all due to your therapy, colonics and the Cayce remedy that put him back on his feet. He threw away all his medicines, and was he happy!!" (Letter attached to reading 5057-1)

Lastly, the invaluable legacy of Edgar Cayce would not even be known were it not for the tireless efforts of stenographer Gladys Davis, the A.R.E., and all of its supportive members. As one member and former Cayce skeptic, Vincent C. Belton, documented in a 1978 communication, "I would like to thank all the dear and dedicated people at A.R.E. whose hard work has made available the information for us who see the tremendous value in the readings." (Addendum to 5057-1)

For me, Edgar Cayce has reinforced some of the most important lessons of life. Humanity exists on this planet to learn and grow spiritually. Each new incarnation gives us the opportunity to pay back our karmic debt and allow our advancement towards the perfection that God seeks in us all. With each cycle of growth, we learn that we are not qualified to judge one another. Each and every person is of equal importance in God's eyes. Even the most hapless, hopeless, homeless person on the street plays a crucial role in the complex university of life—whether it signifies repayment of a karmic debt or acting to help another learn an essential lesson in life. The critical lesson of life always boils down to the same essential and fundamental essence:

...LOVE...

Notes

Preface

1. I continue to offer lectures and workshops throughout the world to promote and disseminate these important concepts. I may be contacted at tbaumann1@yahoo.com.

2. Edgar Cayce Readings © 1971, 1993, 1994, 1995, 1996 by the Edgar Cayce Foundation. All rights reserved.

3. The Edgar Cayce Foundation is the nonprofit organization charged with the responsibility of being custodian of the readings and all related reports and records.

Chapter 1: My Introduction to Edgar Cayce

4. Sugrue, Thomas. *The Story of Edgar Cayce: There Is a River.* Virginia Beach: A.R.E. Press, 1973.

5. Kirkpatrick, Sydney. *Edgar Cayce: An American Prophet.* New York: Riverhead Books, 2000.

6. The Second Council of Constantinople, 553 A.D.

7. Kirkpatrick, *American Prophet*, p. 97.

8. Kirkpatrick, *American Prophet*, p. 525.

Chapter 2: Contemplation on Clairvoyance

9. Baumann, T. Lee. *God at the Speed of Light: The Melding of Science and Spirituality.* Virginia Beach, VA: A.R.E. Press, 2001, pp. 64–65.

10. Brinkley, Dannion, with Paul Perry. *Saved by the Light.* New York: Harper Paperbacks, 1994.

11. A neutral particle, much smaller in mass than the electron.

Chapter 3: The Edgar Cayce Readings

12. For the sake of brevity, I have quoted only a single reading for each ingredient where, typically, multiple references exist.

13. Friel. *Dorland's Illustrated Medical Dictionary.* Philadelphia: W.B. Saunders Company, 1974, pp. 134–5.

14. Friel, John (editor). *Dorland's Illustrated Medical Dictionary*, p. 246.

15. *Iodide* for internal ingestion is currently used for an overactive thyroid. However, *iodine* deficiency causes an underactive thyroid (and goiter) and is treated with oral iodine.

16. Hardman, J.G. and L.E. Limbird (editors-in-chief). Goodman and Gilman's *The Pharmacologic Basis of Therapeutics.* St. Louis: McGraw–Hill, 1996, p. 1317.

17. Insulin was introduced as a treatment for diabetes in 1922.

18. Gladys Davis' entry

19. Friel. *Dorland's Illustrated Medical Dictionary,* p. 1485: The main past uses of strychnine from this reference were as a tonic, a nervous system stimulant, and a circulatory stimulant.

20. Kaiser J. "Sipping from a Poisoned Chalice." *Science* 2003. 302: 376–9.

21. Schwartz, Seymour (editor). *Principles of Surgery.* New York: McGraw Hill, Inc., 1989, p. 1315.

Chapter 5: Examining the Errors

22. Gladys Davis' note

23. Cayce, Edgar Evans and Hugh Lynn Cayce. *The Outer Limits of Edgar Cayce's Power.* Virginia Beach: A.R.E. Press, 1971, p. 58.

24. Cayce, Edgar Evans and Hugh Lynn Cayce. *The Outer Limits of Edgar Cayce's Power.* Virginia Beach: A.R.E. Press, 1971, p. 47.

25. Cayce, Edgar Evans and Hugh Lynn Cayce. *The Outer Limits of Edgar Cayce's Power.* Virginia Beach: A.R.E. Press, 1971, p. 23.

26. Cayce, Edgar Evans and Hugh Lynn Cayce. *The Outer Limits of Edgar Cayce's Power.* Virginia Beach: A.R.E. Press, 1971, p. 23.

Chapter 6: The Radio-Active and Wet Cell Appliances

27. Delany, Dudley. "Therapeutic Use of the Edgar Cayce Radial Appliance and Wet Cell Battery." (http://members.tripod.com/~dudley_delany/index-111.html)

28. Crevenna, R., Posch M., Sochor A., Keilani M., Wiesinger G., Nuhr M., Kollmitzer J., Nicolakis P., Fialka–Moser V., Quittan M. "Optimizing electrotherapy—a comparative study of 3 different currents." *Wien Klin Wochenschr.* 2003; 114(10–11): 400–4.

29. Jarm T., Cemazar M., Steinberg F., Streffer C., Sersa G., Miklavcic D. "Perturbation of blood flow as a mechanism of anti–tumour action of direct current electrotherapy." *Physiol Meas.* 2003; 24(1): 75–90.

30. Sersa G., Miklavcic D., Batista U., Novakovic S., Bobanovic F., Vodovnik L. "Anti–tumor effect of electrotherapy alone or in combination with

interleukin-2 in mice with sarcoma and melanoma tumors." *Anticancer Drugs.* 1992; 3(3): 253–60.

31. Goldman R.J., Brewley B.I., Golden M.A. "Electrotherapy reoxygenates inframalleolar ischemic wounds on diabetic patients: a case series." *Adv Skin Wound Care.* 2002; 15(3): 112–20.

32. Watson T. "Current concepts in electrotherapy." *Hemophilia.* 2002; 8(3):413–8.

33. Kumar D., Alvaro M.S., Julka I.S., Marshall H.J. "Diabetic peripheral neuropathy. Effectiveness of electrotherapy and amitriptyline for symptomatic relief." *Diabetes Care.* 1998; 21(8): 1322–5.

34. Paterson D. "Treatment of nonunion with a constant direct current: a totally implantable system." *Orthop Clin North Am.* 1984; 15(1): 47–59.

35. Paterson D.C., Lewis G.N., Cass C.A. "Treatment of delayed union and nonunion with an implanted direct current stimulator." *Clin Orthop* 1980; (148): 117–28.

36. Dore C.A. "TENS units: electrotherapy is an alternative pain–control method." *Contin Care.* 1990; 10(1): 26–7.

37. Sharquie K.E., al-Hamamy H., el-Yassin D. "Treatment of cutaneous leishmaniasis by direct current electrotherapy: the Baghdadin device." *J Dermatol.* 1998; 25(4): 234–7.

38. Bouter L.M. "Insufficient scientific evidence for efficacy of widely used electrotherapy, laser therapy, and ultrasound treatment in physiotherapy." *Ned Tijdschr Geneeskd.* 2000; 144(11): 502–5.

39. Livesley P.J., Mugglestone A., Whitton J. "Electrotherapy and the management of minimally displaced fracture of the neck of the humerus." *Injury.* 1992; 23(5): 323–7.

40. Cullum N., Nelson E.A., Flemming K., Sheldon. T. "Systematic reviews of wound care management: (5) beds; (6) compression; (7) laser therapy, therapeutic ultrasound, electrotherapy, and electromagnetic therapy." *Health Technol Assess.* 2001; 5(9): 1–221.

Chapter 7: Edgar Cayce on Light

41. Greene, Brian. *The Elegant Universe.* New York: Vintage Books, 1999, p. 349.

42. Eadie, Betty. *Embraced by the Light.* Carson City, NV: Gold Leaf Press, 1992, pp. 86–7.

43. This feature is beyond the scope of this book, but the interested reader may refer to *God at the Speed of Light* for a detailed account.

44. Goodspeed, Edgar J. (translator). *The Apocrypha*. New York: Vintage Books, 1959, p. 191.

45. Matt, Daniel C. *The Essential Kabbalah*. Edison, New Jersey: Castle Books, 1995, p. 90.

46. *The Book of Mormon*. Salt Lake City: The Church of Jesus Christ of Latter-Day Saints, 1981, pp. 178- 9.

47. Dawood, N.J. (translator). *The Koran*. New York: Penguin Books, 1997, p. 249.

48. Edgerton, Franklin (translator). *The Bhagavad Gita*. New York: Harper Torchbooks, 1944, p. 56.

49. Hönigsmann H. "Mechanisms of phototherapy and photochemotherapy for photodermatoses."
Dermatol Ther. *2003; 16(1): 23-7.*

50. Gathers R.C., Scherschun L., Malick F., Fivenson D.P., Lim H.W. "Narrowband UVB phototherapy for early-stage mycosis fungoides." *J Am Acad Dermatol.* 2002; 47(2): 191-7.

51. Dawe R.S. "Ultraviolet A1 phototherapy." *Br J Dermatol.* 2003; 148(4): 626-37.

52. Sep-Kowalikowa B. "Phototherapy as a supporting treatment in depressive patients." *Psychiatr Pol.* 2003; 36(6 Suppl): 99-108.

53. Kymplová J., Navrátil L., Knízek J. "Contribution of phototherapy to the treatment of episiotomies." *J Clin Laser Med Surg.* 2003; 21(1): 35-9.

54. Grundmann-Kollmann M., Martin H., Ludwig R., Klein S., Boehncke W.H., Hoelzer D., Kaufmann R., Podda M. "Narrowband UV-B phototherapy in the treatment of cutaneous graft versus host disease." *Transplantation.* 2002; 74(11): 1631-4.

55. Kawada A., Aragane Y., Kameyama H., Sangen Y., Tezuka T. "Acne phototherapy with a high-intensity, enhanced, narrow-band, blue light source: an open study and in vitro investigation." *J Dermatol Sci.* 2002; 30(2): 129-35.

56. Baldo A., Sammarco E., Plaitano R., Martinelli V., Monfrecola. "Narrowband (TL-01) ultraviolet B phototherapy for pruritus in polycythaemia vera." *Br J Dermatol.* 2002; 147(5): 979-81.

57. Zarebska Z. "Immunologic aspects of phototherapy." *Postepy Hig Med Dosw.* 2002; 56(2): 139-53.

58. Frennesson C.I. "Prophylactic laser treatment in early age-related maculopathy: an 8-year follow-up in a randomized pilot study shows a reduced incidence of exudative complications." *Acta Opthalmol Scand.* 2003; 81(5): 449–54.

59. Kwok A.K., et. al. "Argon laser photocoagulation for the treatment of idiopathic, bilateral, recurrent, diffuse retinal arterial aneurysms." *Ophthalmic Surg Lasers Imaging 2003;* 34(5): 437–9.

60. Ottaviani F., et. al. "Argon plasma coagulation in the treatment of nonallergenic hypertrophic inferior nasal turbinates." *Am J Otolaryngol 2003;* 24(5): 306–10.

61. Bergler W.F. "Argon plasma coagulation (apc) surgery in otorhinolaryngology." *Surg Technol Int 2003;* 11: 79–84.

62. Sampliner R.E. "Prevention of Adenocarcinoma by Reversing Barrett's Esophagus with Mucosal Ablation." *World J Surg 2003-8-15.*

63. Reich O., et. al. "Argon plasma coagulation (APC) for endo-urological procedures: ex-vivo evaluations of hemostatic properties." *Eur Urol 2003;* 44(2): 272–6.

64. Harris J.B., Randle H.W. "Use of the Argon Pumped Tunable Dye Laser for Cutaneous Lesions." www.dcmsonline.org/jax-medicine/1998journals/february98/argonlaser.htm.

65. Chen J., Keltner L., Christophersen J., Zheng F., Krouse M., Singhal A., Wang S.S. "New technology for deep light distribution in tissue for phototherapy." *Cancer J.* 2002; 8(2): 154–63.

66. Macular Photocoagulation Study (MPS) Group. "Evaluation of argon green vs krypton red laser for photocoagulation of subfoveal choroidal neovascularization in the macular photocoagulation study." Archives of *Ophthalmology* 1994; 112(9): 1176.

67. Seidman D.S., Moise J., Ergaz Z., Laor A., Vreman H.J., Stevenson D.K., Gale R. "A prospective randomized controlled study of phototherapy using blue and blue-green light-emitting devices, and conventional halogen-quartz phototherapy." *J Perinatol.* 2003; 23(2): 123–7.

68. Goldberg, Bruce. *Past Lives, Future Lives.* New York: Ballantine Books, 1982.

69. Goldberg, Bruce. *Past Lives, Future Lives.* New York: Ballantine Books, 1982, p. 156.

70. Evans-Wentz, W. Y. (editor). *The Tibetan Book of the Dead.* New York: Oxford University Press, 1960, pp. xxxviii—xxxix.

71. Edgerton, Franklin (translator). *The Bhagavad Gita*. New York: Harper and Row, Publishers, 1944, p. 150.

Chapter 8: Reincarnation—The Life Readings

72. *Revised Standard Version of the Bible*. © 1952 by the Division of Christian Education of the National Council of the Churches of Christ in the United States of America. Used by permission. All rights reserved.

73. Williams, Kevin. *Nothing Better than Death*. USA: Xlibris Corporation, 2002, p. 242.

74. Doresse, Jean (translator). *The Secret Books of the Egyptian Gnostics*. New York: MJF Books, 1986, p. 356.

75. GD = Gladys Davis, Cayce's stenographer from September 10, 1923, to the time of his death in 1945. The brackets in this citation are from Ms. Davis' entries.

76. Eadie, Betty. *Embraced by the Light*. Carson City, NV: Gold Leaf Press, 1992, pp. 89.

Chapter 9: Edgar Cayce Miscellany

77. Sugrue, Thomas. *The Story of Edgar Cayce: There Is a River*. Virginia Beach: A.R.E. Press, 1973, p. 202.

78. Chartrand, Mark R. *National Audubon Society Field Guide to the Night Sky*. New York: Alfred A. Knopf, Inc., 1991, p. 668.

79. Sugrue, Thomas, op. cit., p. 207.

80. The information given in your reading is based upon a reading of the records you have made: (1) In planes other than the earth of 4, 5, 6 and other dimensions. (Our earth you know is a three dimensional plane: that is, we can only be aware of length, height, and breadth.) (2) In other lives here on this earth.

The readings indicate that you have a soul created by God millions of years ago. This soul is made up of mind, spirit and will. The soul lives in the various other planes like Mars, Neptune, Venus, etc., and on the earth in bodies adapted to the surroundings of the respective plane. While in the earth your soul has a physical body, which is like a coat. You live here many times in the course of your development, wearing many different coats.

The Life Reading summarizes all the things you have accomplished in the other planes and in other lives in this earth, describing for you the urges which effect you now, contributing to your development or failure according to the way you use your will.

Notice how frequently the reading mentions the fact that your will, the power in you to choose to do this or that, to say this or that, is supreme over all urges and inclination which may come from other experiences. To be successful in life, to be happy, we all must learn—through experience—how to control these urges and make the best use of them.

Body of the Reading

In paragraph 1 [1261-1 Par. 2] on page one you find references made to " . . . the sojourns in the earth, the activities of the entity in the environs about the earth . . . " You are the entity. This means your individuality, the part in you that makes you entirely different from the millions of other people in this world. Your soul has passed through many experiences like grades in school—it has acquired much understanding and knowledge—just as you do in school. The result—this soul of yours with all its experience—is the entity, it is you. "Sojourns in the earth" refer to your other lives in the earth as described in your reading when you were William Armstrong in New Jersey, Philos in Rome, etc. These are not all of your lives (incarnations) but merely those which influence you most right now. From each of these lives you bring over certain talents and abilities, certain feelings and urges. It is these urges that you must learn to control and use to the best advantage. The "activities of the entity in the environs about the earth" refers to your experiences (your soul's experiences) in the other planes mentioned above. In each of these planes you have a body which is adapted to that particular plane. We cannot understand these planes or these bodies because while we are here in the earth we can only see and feel matter which has just three dimensions. We are unable to see a body such as might exist on Venus because our eyes cannot see fourth dimensional objects, just as we cannot see sound sound [sic] waves—but because we cannot see them does not prevent them from coming into a room and out again—amplified—over our radio. A long time ago people associated these other planes with the planets about the sun, Venus, Mercury, etc. So the names of the planets have come to stand for the various planes of experience through which the soul passes between incarnations. On each of these

145

planes it develops urges and talents, etc., which are expressed here in the earth–plane. (1261–1)

81. Cerminara, Gina. *Many Mansions: The Edgar Cayce Story*. New York: Signet Mystic Books, 1950, p. 31.

82. Brinkley, Dannion, with Paul Perry. *Saved by the Light*. New York: HarperPaperbacks, 1994, p. 58.

83. Kirkpatrick, Sydney. *Edgar Cayce: An American Prophet*. New York: Riverhead Books, 2000, p. 29.

84. Eadie, Betty. *Embraced by the Light*. Carson City, NV: Gold Leaf Press, 1992, pp. 103.

85. Brinkley, Dannion, with Paul Perry. *Saved by the Light*. New York: HarperPaperbacks, 1994, p. 115.

Chapter 10: Windows to God

86. Sharp, Kimberly Clark. *After the Light*. New York: William Morrow and Company, Inc., 1995.

87. Van Pragh, James. *Talking to Heaven*. New York: Signet Books, 1997, p. 3.

Chapter 11: Death, Heaven, and Hell

88. Many near–death victims have reported that, just prior to the traumatic events that jeopardized their lives, their spirits separated from their bodies—sparing them from any pain or suffering.

89. Gladys Davis' note.

References and Suggested Readings

1. Baumann, T. Lee. *God at the Speed of Light: The Melding of Science and Spirituality*. Virginia Beach, VA: A.R.E. Press, 2001, pp. 64–65.

2. *The Book of Mormon*. Salt Lake City: The Church of Jesus Christ of Latter-Day Saints, 1981.

3. Brinkley, Dannion, with Paul Perry. *Saved by the Light*. New York: HarperPaperbacks, 1994.

4. Cayce, Edgar Evans and Hugh Lynn Cayce. *The Outer Limits of Edgar Cayce's Power*. Virginia Beach: A.R.E. Press, 1971.

5. Chartrand, Mark R. *National Audubon Society Field Guide to the Night Sky*. New York: Alfred A. Knopf, Inc., 1991.

6. Cerminara, Gina. *Many Mansions: The Edgar Cayce Story*. New York: Signet Mystic Books, 1950.

7. Dawood, N.J. (translator). *The Koran*. New York: Penguin Books, 1997.

8. Delany, Dudley. "Therapeutic Use of the Edgar Cayce Radial Appliance and Wet Cell Battery" (http://members.tripod.com/~dudley_delany/index-111.html).

9. Doresse, Jean (translator). *The Secret Books of the Egyptian Gnostics*. New York: MJF Books, 1986.

10. Eadie, Betty. *Embraced by the Light*. Carson City, NV: Gold Leaf Press, 1992.

11. Edgar Cayce Readings 1971, 1993, 1994, 1995, 1996 by the Edgar Cayce Foundation. All rights reserved.

12. Edgerton, Franklin (translator). *The Bhagavad Gita*. New York: Harper Torchbooks, 1944.

13. Evans–Wentz, W. Y. (editor). *The Tibetan Book of the Dead*. New York: Oxford University Press, 1960.

14. Friel, John (editor). *Dorland's Illustrated Medical Dictionary*. Philadelphia: W. B. Saunders Company, 1974.

15. Goldberg, Bruce. *Past Lives, Future Lives*. New York: Ballantine Books, 1982.

16. Goodspeed, Edgar J. (translator). *The Apocrypha*. New York: Vintage Books, 1959.

17. Greene, Brian. *The Elegant Universe*. New York: Vintage Books, 1999.

18. Hardman, J. G. and L. E. Limbird (editors–in–chief). *Goodman and Gilman's The Pharmacologic Basis of Therapeutics*. St. Louis: McGraw–Hill, 1996.

19. Kaiser J. "Sipping from a Poisoned Chalice." *Science*. 2003; 302: 376–9.

20. Kirkpatrick, Sydney. *Edgar Cayce: An American Prophet*. New York: Riverhead Books, 2000.

21. Matt, Daniel C. *The Essential Kabbalah*. Edison, New Jersey: Castle Books, 1995.

22. *Revised Standard Version of the Bible*. © 1952 by the Division of Christian Education of the National Council of the Churches of Christ in the United States of America. Used by Permission. All rights reserved.

23. Schwartz, Seymour (editor). *Principles of Surgery*. New York: McGraw Hill, Inc., 1989.

24. Sharp, Kimberly Clark. *After the Light*. New York: William Morrow and Company, Inc., 1995.

25. Sugrue, Thomas. *The Story of Edgar Cayce: There Is a River*. Virginia Beach: A.R.E. Press, 1973.

26. Van Pragh, James. *Talking to Heaven*. New York: Signet Books, 1997.

27. Williams, Kevin. *Nothing Better than Death*. USA: Xlibris Corporation, 2002.

A.R.E. PRESS

The A.R.E. Press publishes books, videos, and audiotapes meant to improve the quality of our readers' lives—personally, professionally, and spiritually. We hope our products support your endeavors to realize your career potential, to enhance your relationships, to improve your health, and to encourage you to make the changes necessary to live a loving, joyful, and fulfilling life.

For more information or to receive a free catalog, call:

1–800–723–1112

Or write:

A.R.E. Press
215 67th Street
Virginia Beach, VA 23451–2061

BAAR PRODUCTS

A.R.E.'s Official Worldwide Exclusive Supplier of Edgar Cayce Health Care Products

Baar Products, Inc., is the official worldwide exclusive supplier of Edgar Cayce health care products. Baar offers a collection of natural products and remedies drawn from the work of Edgar Cayce, considered by many to be the father of modern holistic medicine.

For a complete listing of Cayce-related products, call:

1–800–269–2502

Or write:

Baar Products, Inc.
P.O. Box 60
Downingtown, PA 19335 U.S.A.

Customer Service and International: 610–873–4591
Fax: 610–873–7945
Web Site: www.baar.com   E-mail: cayce@baar.com

DISCOVER HOW THE EDGAR CAYCE MATERIAL CAN HELP YOU!

The Association for Research and Enlightenment, Inc. (A.R.E.®), was founded in 1931 by Edgar Cayce. Its international headquarters are in Virginia Beach, Virginia, where thousands of visitors come year-round. Many more are helped and inspired by A.R.E.'s local activities in their own hometowns or by contact via mail (and now the Internet!) with A.R.E. headquarters.

People from all walks of life, all around the world, have discovered meaningful and life-transforming insights in the A.R.E. programs and materials, which focus on such areas as personal spirituality, holistic health, dreams, family life, finding your best vocation, reincarnation, ESP, meditation, and soul growth in small-group settings. Call us today at our toll-free number:

1-800-333-4499

or

Explore our electronic visitors center on the
Internet: **http://www.edgarcayce.org.**

We'll be happy to tell you more about how the work of the A.R.E. can help you!

A.R.E.
215 67th Street
Virginia Beach, VA 23451-2061